מסורה

ArtScroll Mesorah Series®

Expositions on Jewish liturgy and thought

Rabbis Nosson Scherman / Meir Zlotowitz
General Editors

Gateway to the Talmud

Gateway to

by

Rabbi Meir Zvi Bergman

Translated from the Hebrew by

Rabbi Nesanel Kasnett

Edited by

Rabbi Tzvi Zev Arem

מבוא שערים

the talmud

HISTORY, DEVELOPMENT, AND PRINCIPLES OF TORAH SHE'B'AL PEH — FROM MOSES TO THE BAAL SHEM TOV AND VILNA GAON

Published by

Mesorah Publications, ltd

FIRST EDITION
First Impression ... December, 1985

Published and Distributed by
MESORAH PUBLICATIONS, Ltd.
1969 Coney Island Avenue
Brooklyn, New York 11223

Distributed in Israel by
MESORAH MAFITZIM / J. GROSSMAN
Rechov Harav Uziel 117
Jerusalem, Israel

Distributed in Europe by
J. LEHMANN HEBREW BOOKSELLERS
20 Cambridge Terrace
Gateshead
Tyne and Wear
England NE8 1RP

THE ARTSCROLL MESORAH SERIES®
GATEWAY TO THE TALMUD

ISBN
0-89906-208-3 (hard cover)
0-89906-209-1 (paperback)

Typography by CompuScribe at ArtScroll Studios, Ltd.
1969 Coney Island Avenue / Brooklyn, N.Y. 11223 / (718) 339-1700

Printed in the United States of America by Moriah Offset
Bound at Sefercraft, Brooklyn, NY

Table of Contents

APPROBATION TO THE FOURTH HEBREW EDITION

אלעזר מנחם מן שך
קרית הישיבה
בני ברק

בס"ד יום ג' אייר כ"א למב"י תש"מ

שמחתי לשמוע מחתני היקר ה"ה הרב הגאון המפורסם חו"ב וכו' מוה"ר ר' מאיר **צבי** ברגמן שליט"א ראש ישיבת רשב"י פה בני ברק, כי הוא עומד לחזור ולהדפיס במהדורא רביעית ספרו "מבוא שערים" ובו סדר קבלת התורה והמשך המסורה מדור דור עד תקופת הגר"א זצק"ל, ובו עוד כמה ענינים שהם כמבוא לכל זה.

ולדעתי ראוי הוא ספר הזה להפיצו ברבים אצל כל בן תורה לדעת יסודות אלו, מתוך ספר מוסמך, שממקור נאמן ילכו, כי הרבה חובר בזמן האחרון בענינים אלו, מאלו אשר אין רוח חכמים נוחה מהם, ואין דבריהם מוסמכים בזה.

ולזה באתי בברכתי מקרב לב יהי רצון שיזכה להרבות ולהרביץ תורה בישראל ויגדיל תורה ויאדיר כהנה וכהנה.

מנאי חותנו אוהבו מוקירו
אלעזר מנחם מן שך

3 Iyar, 21st day of the Omer, 5740 [1980]

I was delighted to hear from my dear son-in-law — Harav Hagaon Rabbi Meir Zvi Bergman, Shlita, Rosh Yeshivah of Yeshivas Rashbi here in Bnei Brak — that he is ready to publish the fourth edition of his *Mevo Shearim,* in which he has presented the transmission of the Torah in chronological sequence, from the time it was given on Mount Sinai until the generation of the Vilna Gaon, of blessed memory, as well as other vital and related subjects which serve as a gateway.

In my opinion this work deserves to be disseminated to all students of Torah, so that they may learn of these fundamentals from a reliable source, inasmuch as many authors with whom the Torah Sages are displeased have recently written about these matters, and their work is unreliable.

It is my heartfelt blessing that the author merit further opportunities to disseminate Torah among the Jewish people.

His loving father-in-law,
Elazar Menachem Man Shach

◆§ *Preface*

Mesorah Publications is honored to present Rabbi Meir Zvi Bergman's classic work, known in Hebrew as MEVO SHE'ARIM, *to the English-speaking Torah public. Though he is a modest, gentle man who shuns the limelight, the scholarly community of Bnei Brak, Israel, regards Rabbi Bergman as one of its leading Torah scholars and teachers. His Yeshivas Rashbi is the intellectual home of a select group of gifted Kollel fellows.*

The Hebrew edition of this book, MEVO SHE'ARIM, *first appeared in 1964. Over the years it has gone through four editions. The Israeli Torah community regards this work as an exceptionally fine introduction to the world of the Oral Torah — its history, development, principles, terminology and chain of transmission. Concisely, it provides perspective, order, and clarity. In the course of the translation and editingof the present volume, Rabbi Bergman has graciously responded to many queries, with the result that this volume,* GATEWAYS TO THE TALMUD, *may be justly regarded as a fifth edition, rather than merely a translation of an earlier work. We are grateful for his help and for the opportunity to present his valuable work in English.*

RABBI NESANEL KASNETT, *a highly regarded American* talmid chacham, *translated the work with accuracy and insight.* RABBI TZVI ZEV AREM, *who is familiar to our readers from his work in the ArtScroll-Yad Avraham Mishnah Series, edited.* RABBI AVIE GOLD, *who continues to embellish our publications with his thoroughness and erudition, read and commented on the entire work. Where necessary, these three provided clarification of unfamiliar terms and concepts and added occasional bracketed footnotes.*

We are grateful as well to REB ELI KROEN, *a newcomer to our graphics staff, who is making his mark as a craftsman and lends distinction to the art of book design. The master,* REB SHEA BRANDER, *continues to set the standard of taste and beauty in the production of sefarim.*

We are also grateful to the entire Mesorah staff: RABBI HERSH GOLDWURM, *whose encyclopedic knowledge continues to be breathtaking,* RABBI YEHEZKEL DANZIGER, STEPHEN BLITZ, YOSEF TIMINSKY, MICHAEL ZIVITZ, LEA FREIER, MRS. ESTHER FEIERSTEIN, MRS. MALKA HELFGOTT, SIMIE GLUCK, ESTHER ZLOTOWITZ, *and* MRS. FAIGIE WEINBAUM.

Rabbi Nosson Scherman / Rabbi Meir Zlotowitz

כ״א כסלו תשמ״ו / *December 4, 1985*

Introduction

This work contains the sequence of transmission of the Torah from Moses until the generation of the Baal Shem Tov and Vilna Gaon, selected Talmudic principles, the surnames of the Sages, a short explanation of the thirteen hermeneutical rules by which the Talmud interprets Scripture, and other subjects which serve as an introduction to the Halachah (the body of Jewish law). I have presented only a minute fraction of the relevant material — simple, basic and indispensable knowledge to provide students with an adequate foundation, with God's help.

I have drawn from the following sources for this work: *Seder Olam; Seder Hakabbalah* by Raavad; Rambam's *Introduction to Yad Hachazakah (Mishneh Torah),* the Introduction to his *Commentary on Mishnah; Mevo Hatalmud* by R' Shmuel Hanaggid; *Sefer Hakerisus* by R' Shimshon of Chinon, with *Techilas Chochmah; Halichos Olam* with Rabbi Yosef Karo's *Kelalei HaGemara* and *Yavin Shemuah; Shelah; Sefer Yuchasin; Shalsheles HaKabbalah; Yad Malachi; Seder Hadoros; Shem Hagedolim; Mevo Hatalmud* by R' Zvi Hirsch (Maharatz) Chayos; and *Beshaar Hamelech.* When using these sources I have, for the most part, recorded their exact language. Notations of other sources have been made in the appropriate places.

Although every rule has exceptions, I have by and large chosen the rule which generally applies, feeling it unnecessary to list the exceptions. So, too, in the lists of generations I have mentioned only selected individuals.

Some material has appeared lately on these subjects; yet, the fact that these have been published does not mean that they are acceptable — not only because of the authors' untenable philosophical positions, but also because certain of them have expressed individual views which have no basis in Jewish tradition. For this reason I have written a treatise for yeshivah students based on authentic, traditional sources. May it be His will that we be among those who benefit the public, and may this work find favor before Him.

I offer thanks to all those who have assisted me with their comments and suggestions.

M.Z. Bergman

Gateway to the Talmud

Chapter One
The Chain of Transmission

Moses received the Torah from Sinai and transmitted it to Joshua, and Joshua to the Elders, and the Elders to the Prophets, and the Prophets transmitted it to the Men of the Great Assembly (Avos 1:1).

I. From Moses through the Prophets

Moses

M*oses received the Torah from Sinai,* which means he received both the Written Law [תּוֹרָה שֶׁבִּכְתָב] and the Oral Law [תּוֹרָה שֶׁבְּעַל פֶּה],[1] as *Sifra* comments on the verse אֵלֶּה הַחֻקִּים וְהַמִּשְׁפָּטִים וְהַתּוֹרֹת ..., *These are the decrees, judgments, and teachings that* HASHEM *established between Himself and the Children of Israel on Mount Sinai by the hand of Moses (Leviticus* 26:46): חֻקִּים, *statutes,* refers to those laws which are not clearly stated in Scripture, but are hermeneutically derived (see ch. 13); מִשְׁפָּטִים, *judgments,* to the explicitly stated laws; and the plural term תּוֹרוֹת, *teachings,* indicates that the Jews received two Torahs — one written and one oral; *on Mount Sinai by the hand of Moses* teaches us that the entire Torah — including all its laws, nuances and interpretations — was given to Moses on Sinai.

The Talmud *(Berachos* 5a) expounds the verse, *And I shall give you the Tablets of Stone, and the Law, and the Commandment which I have written, to teach them (Exodus* 24:12), as follows: *Tablets* refers to the Ten Commandments; *the Law* means the

1. [As will be evident from the verses adduced below, the term *Oral Law* includes all teachings of the Torah that are not stated explicitly in Scripture.]

Pentateuch (see *Rashi* ad loc.); *Commandment* is the *Mishnah*[2]; *which I have written* denotes the Prophets and Hagiographa [כְּתוּבִים]; and *to teach them* means the *Gemara.*[3] The verse teaches us that every facet of Torah was given to Moses on Mount Sinai.

The Talmud *(Megillah* 19b) further states that the verse, *And on them was written according to all the words which HASHEM spoke with you on the Mount (Deuteronomy* 9:10), teaches us that God showed Moses fine points of Biblical exegesis,[4] in addition to the later Sages' interpretations of the teachings of their predecessors.

Regarding this verse, we are also taught that Scripture, Mishnah, Talmud and Aggadah — even that which an accomplished student will expound before his teacher — all were previously told to Moses at Sinai *(Yerushalmi* to *Peah* 2:4). Even the ethical teachings in Tractate *Avos* were revealed to Moses at Sinai *(Rav* to *Avos* 1:1).

Many commandments in the Written Torah are incomprehensible without the explicit elucidation provided by the Oral Law. Regarding *tefillin* (phylacteries) it is stated: *and as* טֹטָפוֹת, *frontlets, between your eyes (Deut.* 6:18). Without the oral tradition stemming directly from Moses, we would not understand Scripture's intention at all.

In addition, we find that the Torah openly hints at the existence of a parallel body of law, as in the verse וְזָבַחְתָּ מִבְּקָרְךָ, *and you may sacrifice from your herd* ... כַּאֲשֶׁר צִוִּיתִךָ, *as I have commanded you (Deut.* 12:21). Although the commandment of *shechitah* (ritual sacrifice) is explicitly mentioned in the Written Law, the halachic particulars of its execution are not. The phrase, *as I have commanded you,* obviously suggests the existence of a tradition of comprehensive Oral Law.

Even the commandments which our forefathers fulfilled before the Giving of the Torah were reiterated to Moses at Sinai. All that we abstain from or do today is only because of God's commandment through Moses, and not because the Holy One revealed His will to

---

2. [The Talmud consists of two sections: the Mishnah, which is the collection of laws compiled by Rabbi Judah the Prince; and the Gemara, which explains the Mishnah (see ch. 2).]

3. The *Gemara* contains the analysis of the mishnayos from which the Halachah is derived (*Rashi* ad loc.).

4. That is, the rule that the terms אֶת (a preposition without parallel in English) and גַּם, *also,* indicate that something else is to be included; and that the terms אַךְ and רַק (both meaning *but* or *only)* indicate that something is excluded.

prophets who lived before Moses. That we do not eat flesh from a living animal is not because God prohibited it to Noah, but because Moses taught us at Sinai that God proscribed this practice. Likewise, we do not circumcise our sons because Abraham circumcised himself and the males in his household, but because God commanded us through Moses to perform the precept of circumcision, just as Abraham did. The same holds true for the prohibition of eating the גִּיד הַנָּשֶׁה (a sinew located in the thigh), which was originally issued to Jacob; yet we are enjoined through Moses' commandment. For, indeed, it is said that six hundred and thirteen *mitzvos* were told to Moses at Sinai *(Makkos* 23b), and those enumerated above are certainly included in that figure *(Rambam Commentary to Chullin* 7:6).

A total of 613 commandments were told to Moses — 365 prohibitions, equaling the number of days in the solar year [which intimates that on each day of the year they warn us not to transgress them *(Rashi)*], and 248 positive commandments, paralleling the number of limbs and organs in the body [hinting that each of a Jew's limbs and organs tells him to perform the commandments *(Rashi)*]. The word תּוֹרָה, *Torah,* in the verse, *The Torah which Moses commanded us (Deut.* 33:4), has a numerical value of 611.[5] Add to this number the first two of the Ten Commandments which the Jews heard directly from the Almighty Himself, and the figure 613 is reached *(Makkos* 23b).

Tosefos Yom Tov writes in his introduction: Even though Moses transmitted the Oral Law to Joshua clearly and thoroughly, nevertheless, in every subsequent generation novel interpretations are expounded. This statement does not contradict the *Gemara* in *Megillah* (cited above), which states that the Holy One showed Moses even Biblical interpretations that scholars of later generations would make, since Moses never taught these interpretations to anyone else. This solution is apparent from the *Gemara's* wording, which tells us that God *showed* these to Moses, rather than *taught* or *transmitted* them to him. In either of the latter cases Moses would have been obligated to teach these future interpretations to Joshua, inasmuch as Moses was extremely generous toward his disciple, for

5. [According to *gematria,* the system of numerology in which each letter of the Hebrew alphabet is assigned a numerical value, ת=400; ו=6; ר=200; ה=5, thus the word תּוֹרָה equals 611.]

when he was commanded to rest one hand on Joshua in transferring his mantle of Torah greatness, Moses in fact rested both (see *Deut.* 34:9). Thus, the *Gemara* tells us that God only *showed* Moses, but He did not give him these interpretations as a legacy for Joshua.

Accordingly, every scholar who merits to conceive a true and original interpretation in the Torah is regarded as though he brought down a part of Torah from the heavens.[6]

Nevertheless, every detail and original thought was included in the Torah that Moses brought down from heaven, as we are taught regarding the verse לֹא בַשָּׁמַיִם הִיא, *It [the Torah] is not in the heavens (Deut.* 30:12). Moses said to Israel, 'Do not say that another Moses will bring us another Torah from heaven, for I am informing you: *It is not in the heavens* — that is, nothing of Torah has been left behind in the heavens!' *(Midrash Rabbah* ibid.).

In the introduction to his *Commentary on Mishnah, Rambam* writes that prophecy is not effective in interpreting the Torah and extracting the details of *mitzvos* with the thirteen hermeneutical principles. Rather, what the prophets like Joshua and Pinchas must do in the matter of analysis and logic is precisely what the Talmudic sages, Ravina and R' Ashi, do (i.e., interpret the Torah without the benefit of prophecy).

Already in his lifetime Moses began to promulgate decrees and regulations *(Shabbos* 30a). He did so not in his capacity as a prophet, but on his own initiative, in order to safeguard the Torah, as it says וּשְׁמַרְתֶּם אֶת מִשְׁמַרְתִּי, *And you shall keep that which I have*

---

6. This explanation will resolve the difficulty posed by *Ramban* in *Sefer Hamitzvos (Shoresh* 1): in one place *(Megillah* 19b) the *Gemara* says that God showed the precept of reading the *Megillah* to Moses, while in another place (*Shevuos* 39a) it refers to the *Megillah* reading as one of the commandments to be promulgated in the future, after the giving of the Torah.

See also *Ohr Hachayim* to *Leviticus* 13:37, who seeks to reconcile the contradictory statements of the *Gemara,* which in one place *(Megillah* ibid.) says that Moses was given the knowledge of the entire Torah, including even the interpretations of future sages, while elsewhere *(Menachos* 29b) it states that Rabbi Akiva expounded what was unknown to Moses. He proposes the following resolution:

It is true that all Torah knowledge was bestowed upon Moses and that no other sage can know more than he, and that there will be no original Torah thought from the time of the giving of the Torah until the Messianic age that Moses did not know. Nevertheless, there is one qualification. God taught Moses both the Written and Oral Laws, and with His infinite wisdom implanted the Oral Law within the Written Law. Although Moses knew the entire Oral Law, he was not informed of where each *entrusted you to guard (Lev.* 18:30), which the Sages interpret as an admonition to take measures to protect the Torah's precepts from being violated *(Yevamos* 21a). Among his decrees that are known to us: to remove and distance the Nesinites[7] from the main body of the Jewish people (ibid. 79a), and not to sprinkle the מֵי חַטָּאת, *water of purification,* on the Sabbath *(Pnei Yehoshua* to *Rosh Hashanah 29b).*

Included among Moses' regulations are: (1) the seven days of nuptial festivities [during which the *sheva berachos* (seven blessings) are recited] and the seven days of mourning *(Yerushalmi* to *Kesubos* 1:1; *Rambam, Hilchos Avel* 1:1); (2) the first blessing in *Bircas Hamazon* [Grace after meals] *(Berachos* 48b); (3) the public reading of the Torah on the Sabbath, Monday and Thursday *(Bava Kamma* 82a); (4) the study of the laws of each festival during that festival *(Megillah* 32a); (5) the division of the *Kohanim* (priests) into eight ministering groups *(Taanis* 27a).[8]

Joshua

... *and transmitted it to Joshua,* as it is written, *And you shall put some of your glory upon him (Numbers* 27:20). Our Sages teach us *(Temurah* 16a) that when Moses was about to depart to Paradise, he said to Joshua, 'Ask me (to explain) all the uncertainties you have (in matters of halachah).' He replied, 'My teacher, have I ever left you — even for an hour? [I.e., 'I have no uncertainties' *(Rabbeinu Gershom*

---

of its details was alluded to in the Written Torah. Thus, it became the task of great future sages to pinpoint the sources of these laws in Scripture, giving rise to the books *Toras Kohanim, Sifrei,* etc. (see ch. 3). Therefore, when the *Gemara* relates that R' Akiva discovered interpretations unknown to Moses, it does not mean to imply that Moses lacked such knowledge, since — in fact — all Torah came from him. Rather, it means that he did not know the source in Scripture for every law of the Oral Torah.

7. [The Nesinites (Gibeonites) were Canaanites who disguised and presented themselves to Joshua as a foreign nation in order to avoid destruction at the hands of the invading Jewish army. For deceiving Joshua, they were made into hewers of wood and drawers of water for the congregation and the Altar (*Josh.* 9:27). Their descendants were forbidden to intermarry with Jews (see ArtScroll *Kiddushin,* p. 86).]

8. *Rambam (Sefer Hamitzvos, mitzvas asei* 36) explains that although the concept of separate groups of ministering *Kohanim* is from the Torah, it was Moses who divided them into eight groups.

ad loc.).] Did you not write of me, *but his attendant, Joshua, the son of Nun, a lad, never left the tent (Ex. 33:11)?'*

Joshua instituted: (1) the second blessing of *Bircas Hamazon (Berachos* 48b); (2) the prayer *Aleinu Leshabaiach,* when the Jews entered *Eretz Yisrael,* to distinguish them from the *families of the earth* and the *nations of the world*[9]; (3) and ten enactments when the Land was divided amongst the Tribes.[10]

The Elders

... *and Joshua to the Elders,* as it says *(Judges* 2:7), *And the people served* HASHEM *all the days of Joshua, and all the days of the Elders, who lived long after Joshua, who saw the great deeds of* HASHEM *(Avos d'Rabbi Nassan). Rashi* (ibid.) comments that the Elders were the rulers and policemen over the Jewish people. There is a dispute in the *Midrash (Bamidbar Rabbah* 3:7) regarding who these Elders were. R' Yehudah Halevi says that they were the Levites. R' Berachyah maintains that they were Eldad and Meidad; also included among the Elders were Calev, Pinchas and Osniel, the son of Kenaz.

The *Gemara (Temurah* 16a) tells us that one thousand and seven hundred קַל וָחוֹמֶר, *a fortiori arguments;* גְּזֵירוֹת שָׁווֹת, *language similarities* [both these terms are explained at length in ch. 13], and דִּקְדּוּקֵי סוֹפְרִים, *Rabbinic interpretations,* were forgotten during the

---

9. *Teshuvos Hageonim, Shaarei Teshuvah* §44 by *Rav Hai Gaon. Kol Bo* §16 writes that Joshua composed it when the Jews conquered Jericho.

10. Both the *Gemara (Eruvin* 17a) and *Rambam (Hil. Nizkei Mamon* 5:3) refer to them as תַּקָּנוֹת, *enactments.* They are as follows:

(a)That people shall be permitted to graze their cattle in the woods of other people [See *Rashi* and *Radak* to *II Samuel* 18:6 on the phrase, *in the forest of Ephraim;* although the territory on the east bank of the Jordan River was granted only to the tribes of Reuven, Gad and Menashe (*Num.* 32:32*f.),* since Joshua stipulated that one may graze his cattle in the property of others, and since that forest bordered Ephraim's territory, with the Jordan River intervening, the cattle of Ephraim used to graze there and for that reason it was called *the forest of Ephraim*]; (b-c) that wood and grass may be gathered by all in private fields; (d) that shoots may be cut off by all in all places, even private ones; (e) that a new spring may be used by the townspeople; (f) that fishing with an angle be permitted in the Sea of Tiberias (although it was entirely in the portion of the tribe of Naphtali); (g) that it be permitted to defecate behind a fence; (h) that the public may use private paths at certain times; (i) that one who becomes lost in a vineyard may cut his way through, and exit; and (j) that a corpse of a person whose relations are unknown acquires the right to be buried on the spot where it is found.

These ten regulations are all explained in *Bava Kamma* (80b-82a).

mourning period for Moses, and that Osniel, the son of Kenaz, retrieved them with his learning.[11] He and his colleagues began to collect and organize the laws scattered about the Torah into one cohesive teaching. *Yerushalmi (Shekalim* 5:1) tells us that they were called families of *sofrim,* because they made numbered groups (from the word סָפֵר, *sofer,* [*to count*]) of the regulations of the Torah — such as: *Five should not separate* [terumah] *(Terumos* 1:1); *Five species are subject to* challah *(Challah* 1:1); *Fifteen women exempt their co-wives (Yevamos* 1:1); *There are thirty-six offenses in the Torah whose penalty is* kares [excision; premature death] *(Kereisos* 1:1).

Not always were the particulars of each category located in the same place; often they had to be culled from throughout the Torah. For example, the five who should *not separate terumah* are: (1) a deaf mute; (2) an insane person; (3) a minor; (4) anyone other than the owner of the produce or his agent; and (5) a gentile. The fourth category is excluded by the verse, *Thus you shall also separate (Num.* 18:28), while the other four are exempted by a passage in the portion of *Terumah (Yerushalmi* to *Terumos* 1:1). Because in this case as well as the others they gathered this information from all over the Torah, Solomon called the Sages בַּעֲלֵי אֲסֻפּוֹת, 'gatherers' [*Ecclesiastes* 12:11] (see *Netziv* in *Kidmas Haemek).* The Judges were also considered Elders *(Rashi* to *Avos* 1:1; *Meiri* ibid., and in his Introduction to *Avos).* However, some authorities *(Vilna Gaon;* old version of *Avos d'Rabbi Nassan,* ch. 1) list the order of the Torah's transmission as follows: *Joshua to the Elders, the Elders to the Judges, and the Judges to the Prophets.*

Boaz was a Judge. He and his court declared that one should use the Name of God in greeting a fellow Jew *(Ruth* 4:65). We do this when we say *Shalom,* which is one of His Names *(Berachos* 54a, *Makkos* 23b, *Rashi* ad loc.). The Elders and early Prophets instituted the *Kedushah* of *Uva Letzion* in the morning prayer service *(Tur, Orach Chaim* 132).

---

11. The commentators explain that although Joshua was the principal disciple of Moses, he did not restore the forgotten laws himself, but relied on Osniel, because he did not wish to give the mistaken impression that he was transmitting laws as a prophet of God, just as his teacher, Moses, had. See *Asarah Maamaros,* who states that emergency decrees that were permitted for the other prophets were forbidden to Joshua.

The Prophets

... and the Elders to the Prophets. Eli the *Kohen* (priest), last of the Judges, transmitted the Torah to Samuel, first of the Prophets.

Samuel instituted sixteen groups of ministering *Kohanim* (pl. of *Kohen) (Taanis* 27a). He promulgated the law that a non-*Kohen* may slaughter a sacrificial animal, adducing proofs from the Scriptures *(Berachos* 31b). [It is possible that this was one of the laws that was forgotten during the mourning period for Moses; see *Temurah* 16a.] From Samuel's court came the tradition that only males from Moab and Ammon were unfit to enter the Congregation of Israel, but that females from these nations may be accepted as proselytes *(Yevamos* 77a). However, *Rambam (Hil. Issurei Biah* 12:18) writes that this is a הֲלָכָה לְמֹשֶׁה מִסִּינַי, *a tradition that Moses received at Sinai.*

The Prophets transmitted the Torah one to another: Samuel gave it to King David.[12] David innovated: (1) twenty-four ministering groups of *Kohanim (Taanis* loc. cit.); (2) saying עַל יִשְׂרָאֵל עַמֶּךָ, וְעַל יְרוּשָׁלַיִם עִירֶךָ, *on Israel Your people; and on Jerusalem, Your city,* in the third blessing of *Bircas Hamazon (Berachos* 48b); (3) the obligation to say one hundred blessings each day *(Tur, Orach Chaim* 45).

He decreed that the prohibition of *yichud* (seclusion of a man with a woman other than his wife) applies even if the woman is unmarried *(Avodah Zarah* 36b).

The Prophets instituted that *Hallel* be recited when the Jews are rescued from danger *(Pesachim* 117a).

David transferred the tradition to Achiyah the Shilonite, in whose days King Solomon's court was functioning *(Makkos* 23b).

Solomon instituted: *eruvin*[13]; the practice of washing the hands *(Eruvin* 21b); saying עַל הַבַּיִת הַגָּדוֹל וְהַקָּדוֹשׁ, *on the great and holy house,* in the third blessing of *Bircas Hamazon (Berachos* 48b). He permitted the use of paths that crossed privately owned fields if no

---

12. See *Midrash Shmuel* 22: R' Huna, quoting R' Yose, says that on the very night David fled from Saul, he learned from Samuel more than an accomplished student can learn in a hundred years.

13. [That is *eruvei chatzeiros (Rashi)* — a halachic method by which it becomes permitted on the Sabbath to carry objects from one certain type of area to another (see General Introduction to ArtScroll *Eruvin*).]

produce was growing on them (*Bava Kamma* 81b; *Rambam, Hil. Nizkei Mamon* 5:4); forbade marriage to certain relatives who are otherwise permissible according to the Torah (*Yevamos* 21a); and instituted that the *Bircas Kohanim* (the priestly blessing) be said during the prayers. He also erected two gates in the Temple, one for bridegrooms and the other for mourners (*Pirkei d'Rabbi Eliezer* 17; *Rosh, Moed Katan* §93). Solomon's teacher was Shimi the son of Gera (*Berachos* 8a).

Achiyah the Shilonite transmitted the tradition to Eli the Prophet,[14] who lived in the era of Jehoshaphat's court. They forbade a *tevul yom* [a ritually contaminated person who has immersed himself in a *mikveh* (ritual pool), but has not brought the offering necessary for his complete purification] to enter the camp of the Levites (*Yevamos* 7b).

Elijah further transmitted the tradition to Elisha, and Elisha to Yehoyada the *Kohen* [he was *Kohen Gadol* (High Priest)]. One of

---

14. This follows *Rambam's* view that Pinchas was not reincarnated as Elijah (see *Bava Basra* 121b, *Rashi* ad loc.). However, there is an opinion to the contrary amongst the Sages. In *Malachi* 2:4*ff*. it is written, *And you shall know ... My covenant of life and peace was with him ... the Law of Truth was in his mouth and iniquity was never found on his lips. He walked with Me in peace and righteousness, and he removed many from sin. For the lips of the Kohen will guard the knowledge, and they will seek Torah from his mouth, for he is an angel of HASHEM, the Lord of Hosts.* R' Velvel of Brisk explained these verses according to the opinion that Pinchas was Elijah, as follows: The transmission of the Torah from sage to sage, even after a hiatus of several generations, will nevertheless be transmitted by Elijah, who himself received the Torah for his generation. Thus, *My covenant of life and peace was with him* refers to Pinchas, who received a covenant of peace from God. Hence, *for the lips of the* Kohen *will guard the knowledge,* inasmuch as Pinchas (who was a *Kohen)* will preserve the Torah and tradition for the Jewish nation, and *they will seek Torah from his mouth,* since from him the Torah will be sought and restored to the Jewish people.

R' Velvel's father, R' Chaim of Brisk, explains why Pinchas deserved to be the one who safeguards the Torah and tradition throughout the generations and restores it to the Jews. During the incident of Zimri (*Num.* 25), the appropriate halachah was forgotten, and only Pinchas could recall it. He told Moses, 'I learned from you that if a Jew has relations with an Aramean, zealots may kill him' (see *Rashi,* ibid. v. 7). Moses replied that the one who remembers the law should be the one to carry it out. Therefore, just as Pinchas restored the halachah at that time, it is appropriate that he be the one to restore the law to the Jewish people at the End of Days. Thus, in clear reference to Pinchas, Malachi states, *The law of truth was on his lips* (i.e., Pinchas had immediate recall of the appropriate halachah), and *he removed many from sin* (in that he prevented others from following Zimri's example). Therefore, *the lips of the priest will guard the knowledge and they will seek Torah from his mouth* also in the Messianic era.

his teachings is found in the Mishnah *(Shekalim* 6:5). Yehoyada gave it over to Zechariah, his son[15]; Zechariah to Hosea; Hosea to Amos; and Amos to Isaiah.[16] Chizkiyah and his court functioned during Isaiah's life, and they issued decrees regarding the ritual impurity of idols *(Sanhedrin* 12a; *Rashi, Tos.* ad loc.) and the tithing of vegetables (see *Nedarim* 55a and *Rashi* to *Makkos* 23b). When Sennacherib besieged Jerusalem, Chizkiyah composed the prayer ה׳ אֱלֹהֵי יִשְׂרָאֵל, שׁוּב מֵחֲרוֹן אַפֶּךָ, *HASHEM, God of Israel, turn back from Your flaring anger,* which we say every Monday and Thursday as part of *Tachanun (R' Yaakov of Lisa* in *Siddur Derech Chaim).*

Isaiah then transmitted it to Micah; Micah to Joel; Joel to Nahum; Nahum to Habakkuk; Habakkuk to Zephaniah; Zephaniah to Jeremiah; Jeremiah to Baruch ben Neriah[17] *(Rambam, Introduction to Yad Hachazakah);* until Haggai, Zechariah and Malachi, who were the last of the Prophets and the first of the Men of the Great Assembly, as is stated: ... *and the Prophets transmitted it to the Men of the Great Assembly (Avos* 1:1).

II. The Men of the Great Assembly

The אַנְשֵׁי כְנֶסֶת הַגְּדוֹלָה, *Men of the Great Assembly,* consisted of 120 sages, among them Haggai, Zechariah, Malachi,[18] Seraiah, Reelaiah, Mordechai Bilshan (the Mordechai in the *Book of Esther),* Ezra, Nehemiah ben [*the son of*] Chachalyah, Daniel, Chananyah, Mishael and Azariah. They were referred to as Ezra and his court *(Rambam,* Introduction to *Yad Hachazakah),* since he was the chief judge. They were also called Ezra's groups *(Tanna dibei Eliyahu Rabbah* 6).

---

15. He was assassinated. *Pesichta D' Eichah Rabbasi* 23 states that he was the *av beis din* (head of the Court).

16. His grandson Menashe killed him *(Yevamos* 49b).

17. See ch. 1, section II, that Baruch ben Neriah's disciple was Ezra, who was among the Men of the Great Assembly.

18. There is a dispute regarding the identity of Malachi in the *Gemara (Megillah* 15a). Some contend that he was actually Mordechai; others that he was Ezra. A third opinion maintains that Malachi was his only name. The *Gemara* concludes that in all probability he was Ezra; *Rambam,* however, follows the third opinion.

Ezra was worthy that the Torah be given to the Jewish nation through him had Moses not preceded him *(Sanhedrin* 21b). He was the disciple of Baruch ben Neriah *(Megillah* 16b).

They were called the Men of the Great Assembly because they 'restored the crown to its rightful place.' This refers to the fact that Moses had proclaimed הָאֵל הַגָּדוֹל, הַגִּבּוֹר, וְהַנּוֹרָא, *the great, mighty and awesome God (Deut.* 10:17); subsequently, Jeremiah deemed it appropriate to delete the word וְהַנּוֹרָא, *and awesome,* and Daniel deleted הַגִּבּוֹר, *mighty;* the Men of the Great Assembly then reinstated the two terms *(Yoma* 69b).

They also composed blessings, prayers, *kedushos* and *havdalos (Berachos* 33a). Under the leadership of Mordechai and Esther they instituted the festival of Purim. In addition, they wrote the Books of Ezekiel, the Twelve Prophets, Daniel, and Esther (*Bava Basra* 15). Yonasan ben Uziel's translation of the Prophets originally came from Haggai, Zechariah, and Malachi *(Megillah* 3a).[19] The latter were also the source of many halachic decisions in the *Gemara,* transmitted through the generations (see *Chullin* 137b, *Nazir* 53a, *Rosh Hashanah* 19b, *Yevamos* 16a, *Kiddushin* 43a).

The Men of the Great Assembly taught us that whenever it states in Scripture, ... וַיְהִי בִּימֵי, *And it happened in the days of ...,* the intent is to introduce an episode of tribulation *(Megillah* 10b).

The last of this group was Shimon the *Tzaddik* [righteous] *(Rambam* loc. cit), as the Mishnah states, *Shimon the Tzaddik was among the survivors of the Great Assembly (Avos* 1:2). Others, however, interpret the Mishnah to mean only that Shimon did not live during the first years of the Second Temple in the days of Ezra *(Rashi* ad loc.).

They said three things [fundamental teachings]: (1) Be deliberate in judgment; (2) Raise many disciples; (3) Make a protective fence around the Torah *(Avos* 1:1).

Ezra promulgated ten decrees *(Bava Kamma* 82a).[20] Some opine

---

19. See *Maharsha* (ibid.), who writes that Yonasan ben Uziel was the greatest student of Hillel, who lived a hundred years before the destruction of the Second Temple. Therefore, Yonasan certainly never saw Haggai, Zechariah and Malachi, who lived during the first years of the Second Temple. Rather, the *Gemara* means that Yonasan received the translation from a tradition originating with the earlier Prophets. See also *Meiri,* Introduction to *Avos,* who explains this similarly.

20. They are: (a) to read the Torah during the *Minchah* service on the Sabbath; (b) three men should be called to read three verses of the Torah every Monday and

that every anonymous regulation in the *Gemara* was enacted by him.

The custom of striking the *aravos* (willow branches) on *Hoshana Rabbah,* the seventh day of Sukkos, derives from the prophets Haggai, Zechariah, and Malachi *(Sukkah* 44a).

Among the decrees promulgated by members of the Great Assembly were: Daniel decreed that no Jew may consume gentile oil or wine *(Avodah Zarah* 36a) [oil was subsequently permitted by later sages (ibid.)]; Nehemiah prohibited moving certain objects on the Sabbath *(Shabbos* 123b), but this decree applied only to his generation *(Tosafos* to *Bava Kamma* 24b). Haggai, Zechariah, Malachi, Zerubabel and Yehoshua the High Priest forbade Jews from eating Cuthean bread *(Midrash Tanchuma* to *Vayeishev).* Ezra penalized the Levites by declaring that tithes should no longer be given to them *(Yevamos* 86b).

[The decree regarding the impurity of liquids was enacted prior to the era of Haggai and the Great Assembly *(Pesachim* 17a, *Rashi* ad loc.).]

They practiced what they preached. Just as they taught, *Make a protective fence for the Torah,* they were the first to do so.

The very first mishnah in the Talmud *(Berachos* 1:1) speaks about a protective fence for the Torah — the obligation to recite the evening *Shema* prayer before midnight. Thus the *Mechilta* (*Bo* 6:8) states: Why did the Sages set midnight as the deadline? In order to remove a person from sin, to make a fence around the Torah, and to fulfill the words of the Men of the Great Assembly, who said, *Be deliberate in judgment, raise many disciples, and make a fence for the Torah.*

Antigonus

Antigonus of Socho and his court received the tradition from

Thursday; (c) permanent courts of law should convene in every city each Monday and Thursday; (d) clothes should be washed on Thursday in honor of the Sabbath; (e) garlic should be eaten on Friday; (f) on the day a woman is to bake bread, she should rise and bake early so that there will be some bread to give to the poor; (g) a woman should wear a petticoat (according to *Rashi,* breeches) for purposes of modesty and chastity; (h) a woman should comb her hair vigorously before immersing herself in the *mikveh;* (i) peddlers should travel from town to town to enable women to buy jewelry and other adornments with which to please their husbands; (j) one who has had an emission of semen may not study Torah until he has immersed himself in a *mikveh* (ibid.).

them (*Rambam* loc. cit.). Among the members of his court was R' Eliezer ben Charsom, an extremely wealthy man. It is said of him that he obligates all rich men in heavenly judgment, for despite his great wealth his constant occupation was Torah study. Two of Antigonus' students, Tzadok and Boethus (Baysos), became apostates, and from them came the corrupted Sadducees *(Tzadokim)* and Boëthusians *(Baysosim)*.

III. The Pairs

Yose[21] *ben Yoezer of Tzereida and Yose ben Yochanan of Jerusalem received* [*it*] *from them (Avos* 1:4) — from Antigonus and his court (*Rambam* loc. cit.). Some hold that Yose ben Yoezer and Yose ben Yochanan also received the tradition from Shimon the *Tzaddik,* so that *from them* would mean *from Shimon and Antigonus (Rabbeinu Yonah* to *Avos* ibid.).

They were the first of the 'pairs.' Yose ben Yoezer served as *nasi* [president], while Yose ben Yochanan was the *av beis din* [head of the Sanhedrin (the Supreme Court)] *(Chagigah* 16a,b).

They innovated laws of impurity regarding gentile lands and glass vessels *(Shabbos* 14b).

Yehoshua ben Perachyah and Nitai of Arbel received [*it*] *from them (Avos* 1:6). The former was *nasi* and the latter was *av beis din (Chagigah* loc. cit.). Yehoshua ben Perachyah had a student named Yeshu who strayed from the path of Torah *(Chesronos HaShas* [the censored passages of the Talmud] to *Sotah* 47a). Although the Christian censors assumed the Talmud's mention of this wayward student to be a slur on the founder of their religion, the censors were obviously wrong. For the incident in the Talmud's account took place 120-140 years before the execution of Yeshu of Nazareth by Pontius Pilate *(Meiri's* Introduction to *Avos).* Yochanan ben Mattisyahu, the *Kohen Gadol* — the Hasmonean — and his sons lived in their days.

The Hasmonean court prohibited and imposed the punishment of

---

21. *Rambam* (loc. cit.) refers to him as *Yosef.* He was a *Kohen,* and was called 'the pious one among the *Kohanim.*' He was killed by the Greeks *(Bereishis Rabbah).*

lashes upon someone who takes a gentile mistress (*Avodah Zarah* 36b; *Rambam, Hil. Issurei Biah* 12:2). They instituted the eight-day festival of Chanukah, with its *mitzvos* of lighting candles and giving praise and thanks to God (*Shabbos* 21b). They also began to establish holidays, when the Sadducees were defeated, which are mentioned in *Megillas Taanis.*

Later, just prior to the generation of Shemayah and Avtalyon, the Hasmonean court issued prohibitions against a father teaching his son Greek wisdom, and against raising swine (*Sotah* 49b).

Yehudah ben Tabbai and Shimon ben Shatach received [*it*] *from them* (*Avos* 1:8). There are conflicting opinions in the *Gemara* (*Chagigah* 16b) as to which of the two was *nasi* and which *av beis din.* Shimon ben Shatach's sister was Queen Salome Alexandra, the wife of King Yannai. When Yannai executed all the sages, the world was horrified. Finally, Shimon ben Shatach, through his great knowledge, restored the Torah to its former glory (*Kiddushin* 66a).

He also enacted that every Jewish child attend a school of Torah learning (*Yerushalmi* to *Kesubos* 8:1), and that all a man's property become security for the payment of his wife's *kesubah* [marriage contract] (*Kesubos* 82b).

Authorship of the *Nishmas* prayer, which is part of the Sabbath-morning liturgy and the Passover *Haggadah,* is attributed to him (*Siddur Kol Bo*).[22]

Choni Hame'agel (the 'circle-maker') lived in the era of this pair.

Shemayah and Avtalyon received [*it*] *from them* (*Avos* 1:10). Shemayah was *nasi* and Avtalyon *av beis din* (*Chagigah* loc. cit.). They were proselytes (*Rambam* loc. cit.). *Some of Sennacherib's descendants taught Torah to the public. And who were they? Shemayah and Avtalyon* (*Gittin* 57b).

Akavya ben Mahalalel lived in their generation. It was said regarding him that when the gates of the Temple courtyard were closed while the Pesach sacrifices were being slaughtered, not one

---

22. The verses of the prayer hint at Shimon's name spelled backwards: ש=שׁוֹכֵן עַד; נ=נִשְׁמַת; ו=וְאִלּוּ פִינוּ; ע=עַד הֵנָּה עֲזָרוּנוּ; מ=מִי יִדְמֶה לָּךְ. [The conjunctive ו precedes the phrase אִלּוּ פִינוּ in some versions, such as *Nusach Sefard.*]

among the great crowd of men within equaled Akavya's wisdom, purity and fear of God *(Berachos* 19a, *Rashi* ad loc.).

King Herod ruled in their days.

❧ ❧ ❧

Hillel and Shammai received [*it*] *from them (Avos* 1:12). Hillel was *nasi* and Shammai was *av beis din (Chagigah* 16b). Originally, Menachem was *av beis din,* but he left and Shammai replaced him. Abaye and Rava maintain conflicting views regarding Menachem's fate. Abaye opines that he became an apostate, while Rava holds that he left that high office, in order to serve the king (ibid.).

Hillel and Shammai were the last of the 'pairs' — there were five in all.

The sons of Beseira occupied the highest positions in the Sanhedrin following the terms of Shemayah and Avtalyon. When they forgot one halachah — whether the Pesach offering could be brought on the Sabbath — they searched for one of the disciples of Shemayah and Avtalyon who knew the ruling. When they discovered Hillel, they removed themselves from office and appointed him as *nasi (Pesachim* 66a).

When the Torah was first forgotten in Israel, Ezra came up from Babylonia and reestablished it. When it was forgotten again, Hillel the Babylonian came and reestablished it *(Sukkah* 20a).

The first legal controversy between sages was whether it was permissible to perform the rite of סְמִיכָה, *leaning* by laying hands on the head of an offering on the festivals, during which certain types of work are prohibited. All five 'pairs' wrestled with this problem over a period of two hundred years without resolution *(Chagigah* loc. cit.), until finally the disciples of Hillel and Shammai decided that it was permitted *(Beitzah* 20b).

Yerushalmi (Chagigah 2:2) states: Originally, there was only one legal dispute — regarding the rite of leaning.[23] Hillel and Shammai

---

23. *Tosafos (Chagigah* 16a, s.v. יוסי) dispute this, since we find that David and Saul had already argued whether one who offers to betroth a woman with a small coin and with money that he has already lent her intends to do so with the loan or the coin *(Sanhedrin* 19b). *Tosefos Yeshanim (Yoma* 59b) also dispute this, for the *Gemara* (ibid.) reports the controversy whether the sprinkling of blood on the Altar was done while walking around the Altar or with circular movements of the hand. Further, in *Sanhedrin* (12a) a controversy is related between King Chizkiyah and the Rabbis.

increased them to four.[24] Afterwards, as the Schools of Shammai and Hillel expanded and close contact between master and disciple became increasingly more difficult, the incidence of disagreement in halachah grew and grew. As matters now stand, only the arrival of Messiah will clarify all the uncertainties.

The Schools of Hillel and Shammai disagreed on over three hundred issues. Usually *Beis Hillel* took the more lenient view, except for those disputes enumerated in Tractate *Eduyyos* as the stringencies of *Beis Hillel* and the leniences of *Beis Shammai.*

For three years the schools of Hillel and Shammai argued, each claiming that the halachah conformed with their opinion. Finally, a heavenly voice proclaimed, '... אֵלּוּ וָאֵלּוּ דִּבְרֵי אֱלֹהִים חַיִּים, *Both these and those are the words of the Living God,* but the halachah is like Beis Hillel.' Although each group formulated a true concept of the Law, the latter deserved that the *halachah* follow their view[25] because they were humble and diffident, and because they taught Beis Shammai's opinion as well as their own, even giving precedence to Beis Shammai's rulings *(Eruvin* 13b). R' Judah the Prince followed in the footsteps of his ancestor Hillel, for when he organized the Mishnah he always placed the opinion of Beis Shammai before that of Beis Hillel *(Ritva* ibid.).

Hillel's regulations that are known to us include: (a) The *prozbul,* which allows the needy to acquire loans before *Shemittah* (the Sabbatical Year) by legally circumventing the cancellation of debts that usually take place on *Shemittah (Sheviis* 10:3). (b) An enactment regarding the sale of a house in a walled city. The sale becomes permanent if the purchase price is not returned by the seller within twelve months. Originally, the buyer used to hide from the

---

24. Shammai and Hillel themselves argue on four subjects: (a) Shammai says *challah* [a portion of the dough that is separated and given to a *Kohen*] must be taken from one *kav* of flour and Hillel says from two; (b) Shammai says that nine *kavim* (a certain measure; see ch. 12) of drawn water invalidate a *mikveh,* and Hillel says a *hin* of water; (c) Shammai says that menstruating women do not defile retroactively, and Hillel says they do; (d) Hillel says it is permitted to lean the hands on a sacrifice during a festival, and Shammai says it is not. This fourth dispute predated the era of the pairs. (See *Beitzah* 35a, where a dispute is cited between Hillel and the Rabbis regarding tithing. *Maharatz Chayos* suggests that the Hillel referred to there is the son of R' Gamliel of Yavneh. Nevertheless, amongst the students of Hillel and Shammai the incidence of disagreement increased markedly.)

25. *R' Yoseph Karo* in *Kelalei HaGemara* interprets this to mean that only Beis Hillel deserved to ascertain the truth.

seller on the final day of the twelve-month period, so that the sale would become finalized. Hillel established that in such situations the seller could deposit the money in a special account, break down the door and reclaim his house *(Gittin* 74b). (c) The order of washing a body before burial *(Gilyon Maharsha* to *Yoreh Deah* 352:1). Likewise, Hillel's opinions are found in many rulings of the Rabbis (see *Bava Metzia* 75a, *Beitzah* 35a, et al.).

Hillel and Shammai decreed that a person's hands must be cleansed even for *terumah (Shabbos* 14b, 15a), and also that ritually contaminated metal vessels that were broken and put together again should revert to their prior impurity (ibid. 16a).

When the schools of Hillel and Shammai visited Chananyah ben Chizkiyah ben Garon, they made eighteen decrees (ibid. 13b).[26]

Chananyah ben Chizkiyah and his colleagues, the disciples of Hillel and Shammai, wrote *Megillas Taanis* to commemorate past tribulations *(Shabbos* 13b).

The version of *Megillas Taanis* in our possession is actually a later integration of two earlier works. The ancient scroll written by the disciples of Hillel and Shammai contained only a calendar-like listing of all the fasts and holidays. The narrative of the actual events and of the miracles which were wrought for our forefathers was never committed to writing, but was transmitted orally in the manner of the mishnayos and *baraisos* (see ch. 3). Later, when the mishnayos were allowed to be written, the oral narrative was addended to the ancient *megillah,* which accounts for the mixture of Hebrew and Aramaic in the expanded written version (similar to the use of both languages in the written mishnayos and *baraisos).* This also explains why the names of later *Tannaim* such as R' Yehoshua ben Karchah and R' Yose ben R' Yehudah are found in *Megillas Taanis (Maharatz Chayos, Divrei Neviim Divrei Kabbalah,* ch. 6).

R' Nechunya ben Hakanah lived in their generation. He composed the book *Habahir* on the mysteries of the Torah, and the prayer *Ana Bechoach* is attributed to him.[27] He also composed the

---

26. [A discussion of the decrees appears in ArtScroll Mishnah, *Shabbos,* pp. 391-394.] See *Rambam's Commentary* (ibid. 1:4) that the elders of the Schools of Hillel and Shammai issued thirty-six decrees.

27. The Kabbalists maintain that this prayer was organized according to the forty-two-letter Name of God referred to in *Kiddushin* 71a: The forty-two-letter Name is revealed only to one who is modest, humble, of middle age, and does not anger,

prayers which are said upon entering and leaving the house of study (*Berachos* 28b).

IV. The Tannaim

Hillel's Successors

R' *Shimon the son of Hillel received* [*it*] *from Hillel and Shammai (Rambam* loc. cit.), *and R' Yochanan ben Zakkai received* [*it*] *from Hillel and Shammai (Avos* 2:8).

Rabban Gamliel I, son of R' Shimon, was the first to bear the title *Rabban.*[28] He was called Rabban Gamliel the Elder, just as his grandfather was called Hillel the Elder. He received the Torah from his father, R' Shimon.

From the time of Moses until Rabban Gamliel the Torah was studied only in a standing position. After Rabban Gamliel's passing, man began to be weakened by sickness, and henceforth Torah was studied while sitting (*Megillah* 21a).

Since Rabban Gamliel the Elder's death, the honor of Torah has disappeared, and purity and abstinence have departed (*Sotah* 49a).

He established four regulations for the benefit of the public,[29] and another with respect to one who permissibly went beyond the *techum* [Sabbath boundary] (*Rosh Hashanah* 23b).

Rabban Shimon, the son of Rabban Gamliel the Elder, received the tradition from his father. He was one of the עֲשָׂרָה הֲרוּגֵי מַלְכוּת, the ten martyrs killed by the Romans. The *Gemara (Shabbos* 15a, according to *Rashi* ad loc.) states: Hillel and (his son) Shimon conducted their presidencies during the one hundred years before the destruction of the Temple.

R' Shimon ben Gamliel permitted a woman who must bring five offerings after having given birth five times to bring only one

---

become drunk, or bear a grudge (See *Rashi* ad loc.).

28. *Rabban,* רַבָּן, is comprised of the word רַב, *Rav* (teacher, master), and the final נ, which indicates a greater level, similar to the word רַגְזָן, *an irritable person,* which stems from רֹגֶז, *anger (Siddur Avodas Yisrael).*

29. Three are mentioned in the mishnayos at the beginning of the fourth chapter in *Gittin,* and another in a *baraisa* there.

offering *(Kereisos* 8a).[30] Rabban Yochanan ben Zakkai succeeded him as *nasi* (see section B below).

Rabban Gamliel ben Rabban Shimon received the tradition from his father, Rabban Shimon. He is known as Rabban Gamliel of Yavneh, and lived at the time of the destruction of the Second Temple. He became *nasi* after the death of R' Yochanan ben Zakkai, thus restoring the presidency to the family of Hillel.

In Yavneh he added the blessing, *Velamalshinim (And for slanderers),* to the *Shemoneh Esrei* prayer[31] *(Rambam, Hil. Tefillah* 2:1).

He and his court inserted the fourth blessing, הַטּוֹב וְהַמֵּטִיב, *Who is good and does good,* into the *Bircas Hamazon,* after permission was granted to bury the victims of Betar. (This is discussed at length in *Abudraham* to *Bircas Hamazon.)*

They forbade the consumption of meat slaughtered by Cutheans *(Chullin* 5b).

Rabban Shimon ben Gamliel received the tradition from his father. He was the father of R' Judah the Prince. The principle that the halachah follows all that R' Shimon ben Gamliel taught in our mishnayos, except for three instances (see ch. 9), refers to him, not to the first R' Shimon ben Gamliel.

R' Yochanan ben Zakkai

The next link in the chain of tradition was R' Yochanan ben Zakkai and his students. R' Yochanan ben Zakkai became *nasi* after the first R' Shimon ben Gamliel was murdered. He was the least prominent among the disciples of Hillel the Elder. He knew the entire Scripture, Mishnah, *Gemara,* Codes, *Aggadah,* (the non-legal portions of Rabbinic literature) the rules of hermeneutics, exegesis and numerology, the movements of the sun and moon, the

---

30. Although bringing an offering for each birth is a Biblical obligation, R' Shimon ben Gamliel was lenient, in accord with the verse, *It is time to do for HASHEM; they have breached Your Torah (Psalms* 119:126) [which permits a sage to allow a precept to be transgressed in exigent circumstances; in this case, the price for the required offerings had unfairly risen to an exorbitant amount]. R' Shimon ben Gamliel felt that if women did not bring even one offering, this may lead them to eat consecrated food while still ritually unclean. As soon as he announced his decree, however, prices went down *(Rashi* ad loc.).

31. The *Gemara (Berachos* 28b) attributes its authorship to Shmuel Hakatan, because he was the member of R' Gamliel's court who actually wrote it.

conversations of the ministering angels, the demons, and the trees, parables, the mysteries of the Vision of the Chariot (*Ezekiel* 1), and the difficulties that would later perplex Abaye and Rava [in the *Gemara*] (*Sukkah* 28a, *Rashi* ad loc.).

He issued nine regulations[32] (*Rosh Hashanah* 31b).

Five of R' Yochanan ben Zakkai's disciples were considered among the greatest of the Sages:

(1) R' Eliezer ben Hyrkanos, known as R' Eliezer Hagadol (the Great). His study hall was as large as an arena. One rock was placed there especially for R' Eliezer to sit on. Once, R' Yehoshua entered the study hall and proceeded to kiss the rock, proclaiming, 'This rock is like Mount Sinai, and the one who sits upon it — R' Eliezer — resembles the Ark of the Covenant' (*Midrash Shir HaShirim* to 1:2, *Matenos Kehunah* ad loc.).

When R' Eliezer wanted to establish a law according to his own opinion against the majority of Rabbis, his colleagues voted to excommunicate him[33] (*Bava Metzia* 59b).

R' Eliezer was the brother-in-law of R' Gamliel of Yavneh. He compiled the volume of *baraisos* entitled *Pirkei d'Rabbi Eliezer.*

(2) R' Yehoshua ben Chananya. It is said of him (*Avos* 2:11): 'Happy is the one who bore him!' *Yerushalmi (Yevamos 1:6)* explains that when his mother was pregnant with him, she would go to each of the twenty-four study halls in her town so that the men would pray for her child to become wise. After he was born she would bring his cradle to the synagogue, so that he become accustomed to hearing the words of Torah.

---

32. They are: (a) following the destruction of the Temple, he established that the shofar be blown when Rosh Hashanah falls on the Sabbath, wherever there is a court; (b) after the destruction of the Temple, that the *lulav* be taken all seven days of *Sukkos;* (c) that the new crop of grain should be forbidden the entire sixteenth day of the month of Nissan; (d) testimony regarding the new moon should be accepted the entire day; (e) that the witnesses of the new moon should go only to the assembly house; (f) that *Kohanim* should not pronounce the priestly blessings while wearing shoes; (g) that witnesses of the new moon should be allowed to desecrate the Sabbath only for the months of Nissan and Tishrei; (h) that a proselyte need not set aside a quarter of a shekel to bring an offering if the Temple will be rebuilt, because of the possibility that he will use it for other purposes; and (i) that one need not take the fruit of the vine in its fourth year to Jerusalem, even if it involves only a day's journey, but may redeem the fruit with money and bring that to Jerusalem.

33. *Yerushalmi (Moed Katan* 3:1) explains that although R' Eliezer knew that the halachah requires us to follow the view of the majority, he assumed that the rule did not apply since they acted disrespectfully to him.

Onkelos the proselyte[34] received his translation of the Torah from R' Yehoshua ben Chananya and R' Eliezer (*Megillah* 3a).

(3) R' Yose the *Kohen*, who is praised for his piety (*Avos* loc. cit.). His writings were never found in the hands of a gentile, lest they be carried on the Sabbath (*Shabbos* 19a).

(4) R' Shimon ben Nesanel, who is lauded for being one who fears sins (*Avos* loc. cit.). He was wont to teach: Be careful in reading the *Shema* and reciting the *Shemoneh Esrei* prayer, and do not imagine your prayer as a perfunctory act, but as a plea for mercy and grace (ibid. 2:18).

(5) R' Elazar ben Arach, of whom it was said that he outweighs all the other Sages (ibid. 2:12).

R' Akiva ben Yosef received [it] from R' Eliezer and R' Yehoshua, and from Nachum Ish Gam Zu. His father was a proselyte (*Rambam*, Introduction to *Yad*). The *Gemara* identifies R' Akiva as a descendant of Sisera (*R' Nissim Gaon* to *Berachos* 27a, quoting *Sanhedrin* 25a).

The Holy One said to Moses, 'There will arise a man at the end of several generations — and Akiva ben Yosef is his name — who will adduce from the tips of each letter in the Torah heaps and heaps of laws.' Upon which Moses replied to the Holy One, 'You have such a man, and You give the Torah through me?' The Holy One answered, 'Quiet! Such is My decree!' (*Menachos* 29b).

R' Akiva profoundly understood the mysteries of the מַעֲשֵׂה מֶרְכָּבָה, *Vision of the Divine Chariot* [*Ezekiel* 1]. He entered the פַּרְדֵּס, *'garden' of Kabbalah*, and emerged safely (*Chagigah* 14b).

No man was ever so fortunate or great in Torah learning or wealth as R' Akiva (*Rabbeinu Gershom* to *Bava Basra* 12b).

He was one of the עֲשָׂרָה הֲרוּגֵי מַלְכוּת, ten martyrs executed by the Romans.[35]

---

34. See *Avodah Zarah* 11a, which implies that Onkelos lived in the days of R' Gamliel the Elder. *Hagahos Yaavetz* (ibid.) suggests that the *Gemara* refers to another Onkelos, or, alternatively, to emend the text to read *R' Gamliel of Yavneh*. See *Maharatz Chayos*.

35. When R' Akiva was imprisoned he lacked water with which to wash his hands, and so he decided not to eat, saying, 'Better that I die on my own account than transgress the enactment of my colleagues' (*Eruvin* 21b).

Chelkas Yoav explains that all his days R' Akiva was concerned when he would be able to give his life to sanctify God's Name, thus fulfilling the verse in *Shema: You shall love* HASHEM ... *with all your soul.* This, then, is the meaning of 'die on

He wrote *Mechilta* (see ch. 3), and the book *Osiyos d'Rabbi Akiva* is attributed to him. He composed the prayer, *Avinu Malkeinu* (*Taanis* 25b).

You are Akiva ben Yosef, whose name is renowned from one end of the world to the other (*Yevamos* 16a). The numerical value of מִסּוֹף הָעוֹלָם עַד סוֹפוֹ, *from one end of the world to the other,* is 564, equaling the 564 occasions that R' Akiva is mentioned in the Talmud. Further, the numerical value of אוֹצָר בָּלוּם, *a storehouse with compartments,* a term used to describe R' Akiva in *Gittin* 67a, is 375, signifying that the halachah follows R' Akiva's opinion 375 times, like the expression שָׁעָה עוֹמֶדֶת לוֹ (he was successful, שעה=375). According to a variant reading there (*Tos.* ibid.), R' Akiva was called אוֹצָר בָּלוּס, *a mixed storehouse* (i.e., a mind full of all kinds of knowledge), the numerical value is identical to that of his name, רַבִּי עֲקִיבָא (*Hagahos Metzapeh Eisan* to *Yevamos* loc. cit.).

His Talmudic adversary was R' Yishmael, a disciple of R' Nechunya ben Hakanah (*Shevuos* 26a). During the era of the Temple's destruction, while yet a child, R' Yishmael was captured by gentiles, and R' Yehoshua paid a large ransom for his release (*Gittin* 58a). R' Yishmael was exiled along with the Sanhedrin from Yavneh to Usha, as the *Gemara* (*Bava Basra* 28b) says — *Who are the ones who traveled to Usha? — R' Yishmael.* The *Gemara* enumerates five decrees promulgated by the Sages in Usha[36] (*Kesubos* 49b, 50a).

R' Yishmael wrote *Mechilta* (see ch. 3). The authorship of the book *Heichalos* is attributed to him, and he formulated the Thirteen Hermeneutical Principles (see ch. 13).

---

my own account' — that he was willing to relinquish his great yearning and rather die for a lesser, private cause, in order not to transgress the Rabbinic ruling of washing the hands before eating.

Rabbeinu Nissim Gaon (*Berachos* 57b) writes that possibly R' Akiva's piety exceeded his scholarship, and therefore he was praised for his piety.

36. They are: (1) A father must support his small children; (2) one who gives away all his property to his sons is entitled that he and his wife be supported by them; (3) one should not give more than a fifth of his wealth to charity; (4) a child under twelve years of age who refuses to study should be encouraged with soft words; once the child is older, the father should use a strap or withhold food if necessary; (5) if a woman sells her *melog* (usufructuary) property (see General Introduction to ArtScroll *Kesubos* for explanation of this term) while her husband is living, and then she dies, her husband may seize it from the purchasers.

The following are the disciples who received the tradition from R' Akiva:

R' Meir, who was the greatest among them.[37] His wife was Berurya, the daughter of R' Chanina ben Teradyon. She once learned three hundred laws from three hundred scholars in one day *(Pesachim* 62b). We even find that she engaged in a legal dispute with the Sages *(Tosefta Kelim* [*Bava Kamma*] 4:9, [*Bava Metzia*] 1:3).

R' Yehudah ben R' Ilai, who was given the privilege of always being the first speaker *(Berachos* 63b; *Shabbos* 33a). He ruled on all questions of halachah for the household of Rabbi [Judah the Prince] *(Rashi, Tos.* to *Menachos* 104a), and was praised for his righteousness, being called *one pious man (Bava Kamma* 103b).

R' Yose ben Chalafta. When Rabbi thought to challenge one of the opinions of R' Yose, he said: We are too lowly to dispute R' Yose, for the disparity between his generation and our own is the difference between the holy of holies and the most profane *(Yerushalmi* to *Yevamos* 6:7). Every anonymous *baraisa* in *Seder Olam* concurs with him.

R' Shimon bar Yochai, who laid the foundation for the *Zohar,* which was actually composed sixty years after his death.

R' Nechunya ben Hakanah was the leading exponent of *Kabbalah* (mystical teachings); he wrote *Habahir.* After him was R' Shimon bar Yochai, who composed the *Zohar.* When R' Shimon and his generation passed away, knowledge of the *Kabbalah* became lost. Finally, the Almighty inspired one eastern monarch to order his servants to dig in a particular spot for reasons of financial gain, and they struck a box which contained a copy of the *Zohar.* When the sages of Tolitola learned of the discovery, they rejoiced greatly, and from there the *Kabbalah* was disseminated to Israel *(Shiurei Berachah).*

R' Nechemyah.

R' Elazar ben Shamua, the *Kohen.* Rabbi went to him to be examined and to clarify any uncertainties in learning he had[38] *(Menachos* 18a, *Rashi* ad loc.).

---

37. See page 48, that R' Meir is the author of every anonymous mishnah.

38. Rav called R' Elazar ben Shamua *the happiest of all scholars (Kesubos* 40a, *Rashi* ad loc.). The world had been desolate of Torah knowledge and scholarship

R' Yochanan Hasandlar, who praised himself as one who often attended R' Akiva *(Yerushalmi* to *Chagigah* 3:1). When R' Akiva was imprisoned for engaging in Torah study, which was outlawed by the Romans, R' Yochanan disguised himself as a peddler and passed by the jail, calling, 'Who wants to buy needles?' Hidden in this simple query was a halachic question regarding *chalitzah.*[39] R' Akiva then stuck his head out of the window and innocently asked, 'Do you have spindles?' — which was in effect a coded response to R' Yochanan's question (ibid., *Yevamos* 12:5).

R' Yochanan came from the city Alexandria[40] (ibid. *Chagigah* loc. cit.).

Shimon ben Azzai, whose mind was exceedingly sharp, was wont to say, *All the sages of Israel are, in comparison to me, as thin as the husk of a garlic, except for 'that bald one'* (a reference to R' Akiva, who was bald) *(Bechoros* 58a, *Rashi* ad loc.). When Abaye was in a cheerful mood he used to say, *I am like Ben Azzai in the markets of Tiberias,* which means: I am open and ready to answer any questions, just like Ben Azzai, who lived in Tiberias and was keen and learned *(Kiddushin* 20a, *Rashi* ad loc.).

R' Elazar Chisma, who was an expert in engineering and geometry, could reckon the number of drops of water in the sea *(Horoyos* 10a). He used to say: *The laws of offerings and the laws regarding the beginning of menstrual periods — these are the essential laws; astronomy and mathematics are like the seasonings of wisdom (Avos* 3:23), which means that not only are the clear and unequivocal laws of the Torah superior to the natural sciences, but even the gray areas of Torah, where the truth is in doubt, surpass these bodies of exact knowledge. For in the entire Talmud no subjects are more fraught with uncertainty than the laws of the bird-offerings (in Tractate *Kinnim)* and the accurate reckoning of the menses *(Arachin* 8a) which — in the majority of cases — requires that

---

until R' Akiva came and taught it. Therefore, any of his students who understood the Torah like he did had obviously grasped the halachah, and was aptly called 'the happiest of scholars' *(Shitah Mekubetzes).*

39. [When a childless man dies, his brother is obligated either to marry his widow or to perform *chalitzah* (lit., taking off the shoe). See *Deuteronomy* 25:5*ff.* and General Introduction to ArtScroll *Yevamos.*]

40. *Maharatz Chayos* in *Darkei Moshe* suggests that he was called *R' Yochanan Hasandlar* because he came from Alexandria. However, the early authorities maintain that he was actually a shoemaker, which is the meaning of סַנְדְּלָר, *sandlar.*

the offerings be brought but not eaten because of doubt as to whether they are even required. Nevertheless, these unclear areas are considered essential precepts of the Torah, while exact sciences — such as geometry — are only seasonings to wisdom, just as dessert is of secondary importance to the main course.

R' Elazar, the son of R' Yose the Galilean *(Koheles Rabbah* 11:6). Of him, it was said, 'Wherever you find a homiletical explanation by R' Elazar, make your ears like a hopper to receive his teaching.' He formulated thirty-two rules of Biblical exegesis (see p. 155).

R' Akiva had twelve thousand pairs of disciples, from Gabbas to Antiparas, and all of them died at the same time because they did not treat each other with respect. The world remained desolate [because the Torah had been forgotten *(Rashi)*] until R' Akiva came to our teachers in the South and taught the Torah to them: These were R' Meir, R' Yehudah, R' Yose, R' Shimon, and R' Elazar ben Shamua, and it was they who revived the Torah at that time. All of them (the 12,000 pairs) died between Passover and Shavuos *(Yevamos* 62b).

Rabbi

R' Yehudah Hanasi (Judah the Prince), the son of R' Shimon ben Gamliel, known as רַבִּי, *Rabbi,*[41] was also called *Rabbeinu Hakadosh* (our Holy Teacher) because he never permitted his hand to drop below his belt *(Shabbos* 118b). He received the Torah from his father *(Bava Metzia* 84a), from R' Elazar ben Shamua *(Yevamos* 84a), and from R' Shimon bar Yochai and his colleagues, the disciples of R' Akiva. Rava referred to Rabbi as one who drew water from deep wells *(Shevuos* 7a).

Rabbi used to preface his opinions with, *I say (Rabbi says, 'I say ...'),*[42] an indication of his humility, as the Mishnah teaches: *When Rabbi died, humility ceased (Sotah* 49a; *Horiyos* 14a). Rabbi never issued his opinions as absolute pronouncements of the law, but only that it appeared to him as such, much as today's Talmudic scholars write, *It appears to my impoverished mind (Beis Haotzer).*

---

41. Even though we find Rabbi and R' Judah the Prince engaged in debate (see *Yerushalmi* to *Peah,* end of ch. 1), the latter is actually Rabbi's grandson, who is often called R' Yehudah Nesiah.

42. Found often in the Babylonian and Jerusalem Talmuds and *Tosefta.* (See *Kiddushin* 9b, *Gittin* 38b, 39b, 52a, *Arachin* 17a, 24b, *Taanis* 2b, et al.)

Rabbi and his court promulgated rules concerning the *sikerikon*, Roman soldiers who threatened to kill Jews unless they would give them their property (*Gittin* 55b), and the laws of a menstruant (*Niddah* 66a). They decreed that a student should not decide matters of law without his teacher's permission (*Sanhedrin* 5b). After concluding his prayers Rabbi would add יְהִי רָצוֹן מִלְּפָנֶיךָ, שֶׁתַּצִּילֵנִי מֵעַזֵּי פָנִים וּמֵעַזּוּת פָּנִים, *May it be Your will that You rescue me from brazen men and from brazenness ...* (*Berachos* 16b). We now recite this as part of the morning prayers.[43]

Rabbi was the one who organized and edited the Mishnah.

43. The *Gemara* (ibid.) comments that Rabbi prayed this even though Antoninus had ordered his soldiers to guard Rabbi and to thrash anyone who attempted to injure him (*Rashi* ad loc.).

Chapter Two
Foundation of the Mishnah

From the days of Moses until those of Rabbi, the Oral Law was never committed to writing for public dissemination. Rather, the leading Torah authority of each generation — whether he was the head of the Sanhedrin or a prophet — used to make personal notes of the teachings he had received from his masters, which he then taught orally to the people. These personal manuscripts[1] contained not only the particulars of the transmitted tradition,[2] but also new laws that were promulgated at that time using the thirteen hermeneutical rules (see ch. 13), and which were subsequently ratified by the Sanhedrin.

---

1. See *Shabbos* 6b, that Rav found a secret scroll of the school of R' Chiya. *Rashi* (ad loc.) explains that when one scholar heard another propound a law that was not taught in the academies, he wrote it down lest he forget it, yet kept it secret since it was not supported by the tradition. In *Bava Metzia* (92a), *Rashi* defines *secret scroll* as a personal manuscript consisting of novel interpretations that the scholar had heard and feared he would forget, and which he concealed because of the prohibition of writing down the Oral Law. (See below, where we discuss the permissibility of committing the Oral Law to writing.) The *Gemara* also mentions *the notebook of Ilfa (Menachos* 70a), *the notebook of Levi, and the notebook of R' Yehoshua ben Levi (Shabbos* 156a). In *Yevamos* (49b) we are told that Shimon ben Azzai found a scroll of genealogical records in Jerusalem.

2. The tradition was principally transmitted from teacher to student. Any legal decision or law repeated by a student in the name of his master to his colleagues in the study hall was accepted as if the master himself had uttered it — whether to rely on it to determine the practical law, or to ask on it from a conflicting statement of the teacher. Any legal opinion pronounced by a sage is assumed to have come from his teacher unless explicitly indicated otherwise (see *Yoreh Deah* 242:24).

One who repeats a tradition in the name of the sage who originally said it should imagine that the latter is standing before him, for it says (*Psalms* 39:7) *But in their shadow — a man should walk (Yerushalmi,* end of *Shekalim).* On the other hand, one who did not learn a certain halachah from a sage, but cites it in the latter's name,

Such was the accepted procedure until Rabbi collected all the decisions, laws, interpretations, and explanations that had been heard from Moses (see *Yerushalmi* to *Peah* 2:4), or that the Sanhedrin had innovated, and from this material he composed the Mishnah. He publicly taught this text until it became widely known, written down, and disseminated, thus ensuring that the Oral Law would not be forgotten among the Jewish people. Why did Rabbi not just abide by the status quo? Because he perceived that the level of scholarship was waning, that hardships were approaching, that the power of the Roman government was expanding, and that the Jews were being dispersed far and wide. Therefore, he wrote one uniform work for all, to be learned quickly and not forgotten, and he and the members of his court spent their entire lives teaching the Mishnah to the people *(Rambam,* Introduction to *Yad Hachazakah).*

Writing the Oral Law

Regarding the permissibility of writing down segments of the Oral Law, the *Gemara (Gittin* 60b) states: R' Yehudah bar (*the son*

---

causes the Divine Presence to depart from Israel (end of Tractate *Kallah).* Since the entire goal of our sages' Torah study was to cause the Divine Presence to dwell in our midst, they therefore took great pains not to change, add to, or subtract from what they learned from their teachers.

The disciples highly treasured the traditions of their rabbis. R' Chisda was once holding two priestly gifts of meat in his hand and called out, 'Whoever comes and tells me a new dictum in Rav's name, I shall give these to him' ... When they related to him yet another saying, he exclaimed, 'Did Rav indeed say this? I prefer this second one to the first. If I had another [gift], I would give it to you' *(Shabbos* 10b). On another occasion R' Kahana said to R' Ashi, 'Did Rav really say that?' He then proceeded to learn it from R' Ashi forty times, and then knew it as if he had it in his pocket *(Megillah* 7b). In *Chullin* 18b R' Yosef states: 'I studied under R' Yehudah, who mentioned even the uncertainties of authority.' *Rashi* explains that when R' Yehudah quoted a tradition by someone who was uncertain of the source, he would say: 'I received it from So-and-so, who was unsure if he had received it from So-and-so or So-and-so.'

The disciples not only cherished the traditions they personally received from their teachers, but they were even anxious to know if their colleagues had also heard them. R' Ilai said that he had heard certain teachings from R' Eliezer and he asked all the latter's students, looking for another who had also heard it, but he did not find one *(Eruvin* 83a, *Rashi* ad loc.).

They were careful to quote the opinion precisely, even though a slight variance in wording would not distort the basic ruling. R' Yehudah, the son of R' Shmuel ben Shilas, said, quoting Rav, 'The guests may not eat anything until the one who breaks bread has tasted.' R' Safra explained, 'The statement was: '[The guests] may not taste.' What practical difference does it make? Only to teach that one must *of R')* Nachmani, who was Resh Lakish's interpreter, taught as follows: It is written, *Write for yourselves these words (Ex.* 34:27). It is also written: ... *for according to these words* (ibid.). The first verse implies that the Torah must be written; the second, that it must be taught orally. How do we resolve this? The answer is that words that are written [i.e., Scripture] may not be recited by heart, and the words which are transmitted orally may not be committed to writing.

The rationale behind this admonition is that peculiarities in the sentence structure and word formation of the Written Torah contain many hidden meanings and lessons, and if the verses were transmitted orally these interpretations would go unnoticed. Conversely, since the Oral Law is an elucidation of the Written Law, it can be grasped only if a teacher is present to explain its intent. If it were committed to writing, the possibility of misinterpretation would be likely. For that reason it was given orally to Moses at Sinai. However, once the enemy's evil decrees and the numerous difficulties threatened to sunder the people from their Torah, thus posing a situation of עֵת לַעֲשׂוֹת ה׳, *It is time to do for* HASHEM *(Psalms*

---

repeat the exact words of his teacher *(Berachos* 47a). In fact, for this reason the students retain their learning, as it says in *Eruvin* (53a): *The sons of Yehudah who chose their words carefully retained their learning. Rashi* explains that they were careful to repeat the dictum exactly as the teacher had uttered it.

The Mishnah *(Parah* 2:5) teaches, *If [the red cow] has two black or white hairs in one guma (cavity), it is unfit. R' Yehudah says: 'In one* kos.' *Rav* (ad loc.) explains that although there is no halachic dispute between the first *Tanna* and R' Yehudah — since *guma* and *kos* have the identical meaning — nevertheless, they used different expressions because each was obligated to repeat the exact language of his teacher. Also, the *Gemara* in *Shabbos* (15a) states that Hillel said: *A* hin *of drawn water invalidates the* mikveh, for one must state a halachah using his teacher's exact phraseology (see *Rashi* there). However, *Rambam* in his *Mishnah Commentary* to *Eduyyos* (1:3) writes that he received a tradition from his teacher, and *Rambam's* teacher from his teacher, that Hillel's masters, the proselytes Shemayah and Avtalyon, because of their inability to enunciate the letter ה *(he)* correctly, pronounced it as an א *(alef)*. Thus, when they said the dictum: *a* hin *of drawn water invalidates the* mikveh, it sounded like *drawn water does* not *invalidate* (the word הִין, *hin,* sounded like אֵין, *does not).* Hillel — who could certainly pronounce the letter *he* — nevertheless employed the phraseology of his teachers. *Vilna Gaon* explains *Rambam's* meaning as follows: Since their inability to pronounce the *he* in *hin* could very well cause people to think mistakenly that drawn water does not invalidate a *mikveh,* Shemayah and Avtalyon were forced to use the word מְלֹא, *the amount of,* before the word *hin*. Hillel, who could say *hin* correctly, did not need to add the extra word. Yet, he did so in order to repeat the ruling in his teacher's exact wording. Thus, the most basic principle of the transmission of the Oral Law from teacher to student is precision of language.

119:126), the Sages were compelled to permit the recording of the Oral Law — הֵפֵרוּ תּוֹרָתֶךָ, *they breached Your Torah* (ibid.).[3]

The early authorities were divided as to whether Rabbi was the one who authorized the writing of the Mishnah. *Rambam* maintains that he was; however, *Rashi* contends that while Rabbi arranged the mishnayos and taught them orally, he never wrote them down.[4]

Earlier Mishnayos

Actually, long before Rabbi, efforts had been made to compile and arrange the mishnayos (*Chagigah* 14a). R' Yehudah ben Teima and his colleagues taught six hundred orders of mishnayos (some maintain that it was seven hundred), and Rabbi subsequently reduced them to six orders. However, a responsum from *R' Sherira Gaon* seems to indicate that Hillel and Shammai fashioned the six orders and that Rabbi only edited and refined them, ultimately producing the work that we have today (*Shem Hagedolim*).[5]

---

3. Similarly, the Sages permitted recitation of the Written Torah on certain occasions. For example, the *Kohen Gadol* (High Priest) read one section of the Torah by heart (*Yoma* 68b) so as not to trouble the assembly [by having them wait until the Scroll was turned to that portion] (ibid. 70a). See *Tosafos (Temurah* 14b), that the prohibition against reciting the Written Torah applied basically to cases in which one person was reading on behalf of others.

4. See *Eruvin* 62b, where the *Gemara* refers to *Megillas Taanis* as having been written and *Rashi* explains that the *Gemara* specifies *Megillas Taanis* because other than that work, not even one letter of a statement of halachah appeared in written form in those days (see page 33).

In the period of the sages of the *Gemara*, during the lifetime of Abaye, the Mishnah had not yet appeared in writing. Evidence is adduced from *Eruvin* 53a and *Avodah Zarah* 2a, where the spelling of certain terms in the Mishnah are disputed. Had the Mishnah already been committed to writing, they could have simply looked up the spelling.

Further, the *Gemara (Bava Metzia* 85b) reports how R' Chiya orally taught the six orders of the Mishnah to six schoolchildren, whereas he taught the five books of the Torah to five youngsters from a text. From here we see that in the time of R' Chiya, who was a disciple of Rabbi, the mishnayos were still taught orally.

However, in defense of *Rambam's* opinion, it might be said that the written Mishnah was not yet widely disseminated, and that whoever was still capable of learning it by heart continued to do so, since permission to write it down had been granted only out of great necessity.

5. See *Teshuvos Hageonim* §20 by *R' Hai Gaon*, who writes that from the days of Moses until Hillel the Elder six hundred orders of the Mishnah were extant, just as the Holy One had given them to Moses at Sinai. From Hillel onward the general condition of the world deteriorated, and the honor of Torah diminished, and so Hillel and Shammai established only six orders.

Many tractates of mishnayos were arranged by others before Rabbi, such as *Middos* by R' Eliezer ben Yaakov and the entire tractate *Kelim (Chacham Tzvi).* Wherever it says in the Mishnah, *even though they said,* or *and why did they say,* or *because they said (Pesachim* 1:1, *Shabbos* 1:3, et al.), reference is being made to these earlier mishnayos, which is also the intent of the *Gemara* when it mentions a *mishnah rishonah* [earlier mishnah] and *mishnah achronah* [later mishnah] *(Kesubos* 57a, *Sanhedrin* 27b). We also find in the *Gemara: This mishnah was taught in the days of Nehemiah ben Chachalyah* (see page 26).

The first three mishnayos in *Bava Kamma* are unique in their brevity and style. The *Gemara* there (6b) comments, 'that *Tanna* is a *Yerushalmi,*' which means that those mishnayos were composed by a sage from Jerusalem who chose to write concisely, and Rabbi subsequently included them — unedited — in his mishnayos *(Maharatz Chayos* ibid.).[6]

Tiferes Yisrael (*Makkos* 3:3, *Zevachim* 5:3) comments on the mishnah concerning offerings that are eaten within the 'curtains' of the Temple (i.e., within the Temple enclosure), that the word

---

6. My good friend, Harav Shlomo Min Hahar *shlita,* suggests that from the style of the mishnayos in the fourteenth chapter of *Zevachim* it appears that their intent was to teach practical halachah and, apparently, they predated Rabbi. Also, the mishnayos which teach the laws of *Yovel* (the Jubilee, or fiftieth year) must have been disseminated before Chizkiyah, in whose time celebration of *Yovel* was discontinued (this, according to *Rashi,* who maintains that *Yovel* was not observed during the Second Temple period).

Even more convincing is the *Gemara* in *Gittin* (48a), which dates the mishnayos concerning first fruits *(bikkurim)* from the time of the first *Yovel,* and *Rashi* (ad loc.) understands this to mean the first *Yovel* the Jewish nation ever observed — in the days of Joshua (see *Meiri* ibid.). Thus, we have clear proof that mishnayos were taught as early as Joshua's time, for since then the laws of *bikkurim* have changed; nevertheless, the original formulation has been retained.

Similarly, *Ohr HaChaim* on the Torah writes that the *baraisa* in *Shabbos* 6b, *Which is a public domain? A highroad, a great open space, open alleys and the desert,* was originally taught when the Jews were in the Desert (but see, however, *Metzapeh Eisan* there, who avers that the *baraisa* only means if 600,000 men were to walk in the desert today). Also, mishnayos whose meanings were subsequently interpreted differently by other *Tannaim* (sages of the Mishnah) most probably were written earlier (see *Peah* 4:5, *Kelaim* 2:1,2, et al.). It happened that once the *Kohen Gadol* prolonged his prayer. They said to him, 'Do not make a habit of doing so, for we have learned: *He would not pray long, lest he terrify Israel* — which is a mishnah *(Yoma* 53b). Thus, we see that already in the era of the Temple the mishnayos were being taught. See *Maharatz Chayos* to *Shabbos* (12b), quoting *Vilna Gaon.*

curtains which was dictated to Moses by the Almighty was used in the Mishnah because in Moses' day — when this mishnah was taught — the walls of the Tabernacle were indeed made of curtains, and every mishnah regarding which there is no dispute between *Tannaim* (sages of the Mishnah) has been taught in the exact language that Moses said it. For this reason we read this chapter of *Zevachim* — *Aizehu Mekoman* — each day, as part of the morning prayers, because there are no disputes regarding it, and so it has retained its original formulation.

R' Nassan, who lived in the generation preceding Rabbi's, also compiled many mishnayos, as it says: *This is the mishnah of R' Nassan.* This is the meaning of *Rabbi and R' Nassan conclude the Mishnah (Bava Metzia* 86b; see *Maharsha* ad loc.) — that is, R' Nassan was the last compiler of the mishnayos before Rabbi.

R' Sherira Gaon writes in one of his letters that Rabbi edited some mishnayos, while preserving others in their original form. Anonymous mishnayos reflect the opinion of R' Meir. As R' Meir learned the subject and taught it to his students, so did Rabbi establish the lesson as a mishnah, for R' Meir was the greatest of R' Akiva's disciples, as the *Gemara (Eruvin* 13b) states: *R' Acha ben Chanina said: It is revealed and known before Him Who spoke and the world came into existence that in the generation of R' Meir there was none equal to him. Why, then, was the halachah not decided according to his views? Because his colleagues could not fathom the depths of his reasoning, for he would declare the ritually impure to be pure and adduce adequate proof, and the ritually pure to be impure and also supply proof.*

Therefore, R' Akiva regarded R' Meir very fondly, even supporting him in his youth, and Rabbi adopted his style of teaching — which corresponded to R' Akiva's — in the Mishnah, because it was succinct, lucid, cohesive, and far more precise than those of his colleagues, conveying the desired thought with neither too many nor too few words. Each word that he did select was laden with marvelous implications, which not every sage could fathom. Even though all the *Tannaim* could reason equally well, R' Meir's opinions were preferred to those of his colleagues; therefore, Rabbi selected them, and added later contemporary decisions.

He also cited individual opinions which are not followed by the halachah, so that if one should claim it for a support, he can be told that it is a minority opinion and not according to the accepted law (*Eduyyos* 1:6).

Omissions in the Mishnah

Often the *Gemara* comments that a mishnah is חַסּוּרֵי מִיחַסְּרָא, *deficient.* The *Gemara* does not mean to imply that the omission is a defect in the text, but that Rabbi intentionally deleted that which could otherwise be inferred. That is, since writing down the Oral Law was permitted only because of extreme necessity *(It is time to do for HASHEM),* Rabbi was constrained to do so as infrequently as possible. Where he could rely on the student to understand the mishnah's full import without the missing phrases, he was not permitted to write them.[7]

Some opine that Rabbi's omissions were based on mystical considerations, and they bring support for this view *(Sefer Habris).*

The disciples of *Vilna Gaon* wrote that their teacher knew all the omissions in the Talmud and did not consider them omissions at all. Rabbi would not have omitted anything from the mishnayos. Rather, the intent is that Rabbi followed the opinion of one *Tanna,* and composed the particular mishnah accordingly. The *Gemara,* however, agreed with another disputing *Tanna,* and wished to reconcile the mishnah according to him. This was done by adding words to the mishnah (Introduction to *Pe'as Hashulchan; Aliyos Eliyahu).*

The later commentators note that the *Gemara's* expression וְכָךְ תָּנֵי, *include such and such,* is not synonymous with *the Mishnah is deficient.* Rather, the former means that you should not actually insert it in the text, yet this is its implication, and the *Tanna* had his reasons for leaving it out *(Yad Malachi,* quoting *Drishah;* but see *Rashi* to *Zevachim* 114b, who does explain this expression to mean *the Mishnah is deficient).*

Language

The Mishnah was written in the Hebrew language. *Rambam* attests to Rabbi's clarity of expression, commenting that he was the

7. I have heard this explanation from others [see *Pachad Yitzchak* on Chanukah, *Maamar* 1]. To be sure, it follows only *Rambam's* view that Rabbi committed Mishnah to writing (see above). *Shelah* quotes *She'eiris Yosef,* who quotes *R' Mattisyahu of France,* that Rabbi wrote the Mishnah very concisely, and one can understand the full intent of the *Tanna* from what appears in the mishnah alone.

most gifted writer in the Holy Language. The Sages even resolved their difficulty understanding obscure words in Scripture by listening to Rabbi's servants speak (see *Megillah* 18a, *Rosh Hashanah* 26b). *R' Sherira Gaon* wrote that Rabbi wrote clearly and succinctly, so that each word was pregnant with an untold number of interpretations and legal implications. His work was obviously accomplished with Divine assistance.

The Tractates

The division of the Six Orders of the Mishnah into individual tractates was apparently undertaken by Rabbi, for originally there were six or seven hundred orders, as noted above, whereas now we have a total of only sixty-one tractates. Even though the earlier orders were also divided into tractates, as seen in the episode of R' Meir and R' Nassan concerning Tractate *Uketzin (Horayos* 13b), Rabbi nevertheless reorganized them into tractates within the framework of six orders.

The Hebrew word for tractate — מַסֶּכֶת, *masseches* [the Aramaic form מַסֶּכְתָּא is often heard in common speech] — derives from מָסְכָה יֵינָהּ, *diluted her wine (Proverbs* 9:2), for each tractate contains a mixture of disparate laws. The preceding verse there states: *She (Wisdom) has hewn out her seven pillars,* which the *Gemara (Shabbos* 116a) interprets to mean the seven books of the Torah.[8] Thus, the Oral Law *dilutes the wine* and *arranges the table* (loc. cit.) of the Written Law, for without the oral tradition no man would dare approach the Written Torah. *Dilutes the wine* has yet another interpretation: that the various laws and ordinances of the Torah are mixed and bound to one another so that a law of one subject may be deduced from one in another area, or that one rule may be explained or clarified by another. That is why a group of chapters of the Mishnah is called מַסֶּכֶת, from the word מְסִיכָה, *mixture,* just as the word גְּבִירָה, *rich lady,* is related to גְּבֶרֶת, *lady* (Introduction to *Tos. Yom Tov).*

Others explain that *masseches* means *weaving,* like עִם הַמַּסָּכֶת, *with the web (Judges* 16:13), in the story of Samson. Thus, the Oral

---

8. [The passage *Vayehi Binsoa* ... *(Num.* 10:35-36) is considered a book unto itself, thus dividing *Numbers* into three books, giving the Torah a total of seven books (*Gem.* ad loc.).]

Law resembles fibers such as wool or flax, which one labors to weave into a cogent entity (*Sefer Chasidim*, ch. 928).[9]

Still others interpret that the Mishnah represents the warp of the loom and the *Gemara* the woof, for the *Gemara* is the 'soul' of the tractate, since one may not decide the law from the Mishnah alone (*Tos. Anshei Shem*).

Alternatively, *masseches* derives from מָסָךְ, *masach*, screen in front of the door (see *Ex.* 26:36, et al.), since the Oral Law is the door through which one enters the Written Law (*Sefer Leket Hakemach*). Another interpretation is that *masseches* stems from כִּיסוּי, *a covering*, to teach us that the Mishnah is hidden and not fathomable without the *Gemara* (*Tos. Anshei Shem*). Also, the numerical value of מַסֶּכֶת is 520; if we add four for the number of letters in the word, the total is 524, equaling the number of chapters in the Mishnah (*Chida*).[10]

The tractates are titled according to their subject matter, but occasionally the name is taken from the first word of the opening mishnah, as in Tractate *Beitzah*. Indeed, some refer to it as Tractate *Yom Tov* because it discusses the laws of the Festivals.

The rule is that in regard to two different tractates there is no order to the mishnayos. Thus, if a mishnah containing a dispute between *Tannaim* appears in one tractate, and another mishnah without a dispute and contradicting one of the opinions in the first mishnah appears in a later tractate, we do not say that the halachah follows the second mishnah, as we would if both appeared in the same tractate (see page 92). This is because Rabbi did not teach the tractates in any particular order, but only according to the interests of his students. However, the final composition of the mishnah was done in a certain order, and therefore explanations must be given as

---

9. *Tosefos Anshei Shem* demur, arguing that *masseches* refers not to weaving, but to the warp of the loom, which is tightly wound around the pole. However, perhaps we can still say that *masseches* implies something arranged or in one place, and such was the intent of *Sefer Chassidim*.

10. [A well-known mnemonic device for this number is that it is the numerical value of תַּלְמוּד בַּבְלִי, *the Babylonian Talmud*, although, of course, the Mishnah is the same in the Jerusalem Talmud as well.] However, in his Introduction to *Yad*, *Rambam* states that the Mishnah contains only 523 chapters. Further, one should know that the fourth chapter of Tractate *Bikkurim* consists of *baraisos*, not mishnayos; likewise, the sixth chapter of *Avos*.

to why each tractate occupies its position in its order (first *Tosafos* to *Bava Metzia).*

Regarding the Six Orders themselves (i.e., the mishnah with the dispute appears in a tractate in one order, and the mishnah without a dispute appears in a later order), some hold that Rabbi taught them in a specific order, and therefore we apply the principle that when a mishnah containing a dispute is followed by one expressing only one opinion on the same subject, the halachah follows the second mishnah *(Kesef Mishneh, Hil. Rotzeach).* Others, however, maintain that even regarding the Orders there is no real arrangement *(Tos.* to *Shabbos* 81b).

The Six Orders of the Mishnah are: (1) זְרָעִים, *Zeraim* (seeds; dealing with agricultural laws), (2) מוֹעֵד, *Moed* (festival), (3) נָשִׁים, *Nashim* (women), (4) נְזִיקִין, *Nezikin* (damages), (5) קָדָשִׁים, *Kodashim* (consecrated items), and (6) טַהֲרוֹת, *Taharos* (ritual purities). The mnemonic acronym is זְמַן נְקַט, *hold on to time* [which implies an appeal to the Jews to recognize and to uphold the Oral Law in all times *(Abarbanel)*].

The *Gemara (Shabbos* 31a) teaches: What is meant by the verse, *There shall be faith in your times, strength, salvation, wisdom and knowledge (Isaiah* 33:6)? *Faith* refers to Zeraim;[11] *your times* to Moed; *strength* to Nashim[12]; *salvation* to Nezikin[13]; *wisdom* to Kodashim; and *knowledge* to Taharos. Yet, even so, the verse concludes: *the fear of the Lord is his treasure.* The *sine qua non* of all Torah knowledge is the fear of God; without it, there is nothing (see *Maharatz Chayos* to *Shabbos* loc. cit., quoting *Vilna Gaon; Ohr HaChaim* to *Deut.* 13:5).

The *Midrash* (to *Song of Songs* 6:8) says: *Sixty are royalty* — these are the sixty orders of halachos, which refers to the sixty tractates,[14] and they are:

---

11. *Rashi* explains that only the man of faith will tithe his produce properly. *Tosafos* cite *Yerushalmi* that it is so called because one should sow with faith in the Almighty.

12. *Rashi* renders this word in the verse as *heirs,* who, of course, are born from women. I have heard that the Order of *Nashim* is called *strength,* for indeed it is the strength and the shelter of the Jewish people, since it basically discusses Jewish family life.

13. *Rashi* explains that *Nezikin* helps people by admonishing them not to injure one another, and thereby bring financial obligations upon themselves.

14. See page 78, that one who knew all sixty tractates was worthy of the title גָּאוֹן,

Zeraim includes: (1) *Berachos,* (2) *Peah,* (3) *Demai,* (4) *Kilaim,* (5) *Sheviis,* (6) *Terumos,* (7) *Maasros,* (8) *Maaser Sheni,* (9) *Challah,* (10) *Orlah,* (11) *Bikkurim.* Some count *Maasros* and *Maaser Sheni* as one, in which case the total is ten.

Moed includes: (1) *Shabbos,* (2) *Eruvin,* (3) *Pesachim,* (4) *Shekalim,* (5) *Yoma,* (6) *Sukkah,* (7) *Beitzah,* (8) *Rosh Hashanah,* (9) *Taanis,* (10) *Megillah,* (11) *Moed Katan,* (12) *Chagigah.*

Nashim contains: (1) *Yevamos,* (2) *Kesubos,* (3) *Nedarim,* (4) *Nazir,* (5) *Sotah,* (6) *Gittin,* (7) *Kiddushin.*

Nezikin contains: (1) *Bava Kamma,* (2) *Bava Metzia,* (3) *Bava Basra,* (4) *Sanhedrin,* (5) *Makkos,* (6) *Shevuos,* (7) *Eduyos,* (8) *Avodah Zarah,* (9) *Avos,* (10) *Horayos.* However, some consider *Bava Kamma, Bava Metzia* and *Bava Basra* as one long tractate, which would reduce the total to eight. Others consider *Sanhedrin* and *Makkos* as one, further lowering the figure to seven tractates.[15]

Kodashim includes: (1) *Zevachim,* (2) *Menachos,* (3) Chullin, (4) *Bechoros,* (5) *Arachin,* (6) *Temurah,* (7) *Kereisos,* (8) *Me'ilah,* (9) *Tamid,* (10) *Middos,* (11) *Kinnim.*

Taharos contains: (1) *Kelim,*[16] (2) *Ohalos,* (3) *Negaim,* (4) *Parah,* (5) *Taharos,* (6) *Mikvaos,* (7) *Niddah,* (8) *Machshirin,* (9) *Zavim,* (10) *Tevul Yom,* (11) *Yadayim,* (12) *Uketzin.*

The term *mishnah* is similar to מִשְׁנֶה לַמֶּלֶךְ, *mishneh lamelech* (deputy to a king) [*Esther* 10:3], since the Written Torah is the king and the Mishnah is subordinate to it. *Mishnah* also means to teach; hence, the masters of the Mishnah are called תַּנָּאִים, *Tannaim,* which is the Aramaic equivalent of teachers,[17] since they taught us the Mishnah.

The Rabbis of the *Gemara* are called אֲמוֹרָאִים, *Amoraim,* since

---

gaon, whose numerical value is sixty. Regarding the exact number of the tractates, it will be seen in the listing below that there are different ways of listing the tractates, which can yield a total of 60, 61, or 63. See also footnote there.

15. *Ri Migash* and *Ritva* opine that those who consider all of *Nezikin* as one tractate refer to the entire Order and not just the three *'Bavas.'* According to this opinion, *Nezikin* contains just one tractate. See *Yad Malachi* §338. See *Maharsha* to *Tosafos, Bava Basra* 2a s.v. השותפין.

16. In the *Tosefta,* Tractate *Kelim* is divided into three parts — *Bava Kamma, Bava Metzia* and *Bava Basra* — just as *Nezikin,* according to the opinion that it is one tractate.

17. וְשִׁנַּנְתָּם, *and you shall teach them (Deut.* 6:7), is translated by Onkelos as ותְתָנֵינוּן, of the same root as תַּנָּאִים.

after the Mishnah was finalized no one was allowed to add to or subtract from it in any way. The later sages were permitted only to explain and interpret the mishnayos as they had been taught by their teachers. *Amora* means interpreter in Aramaic.[18]

The students of Rabbi who accepted the tradition from him were: his sons, Shimon and Gamliel, as well as R' Efes, R' Chanina bar Chama, R' Chiya, R' Yannai, Bar Kappara, Rav, Shmuel, R' Yochanan (according to *Rambam)*, Levi, R' Bisa, and (according to *Ravad)* R' Chama.

18. As we find in the *Gemara:* Place an *amora* [interpreter] by his side *(Gittin* 43a, *Rashi* ad loc.; *Chullin* 100a; et al.).

Chapter Three
Sifra, Sifrei, Tosefta, Baraisos, and Mechilta

Rav compiled the *Sifra* and the *Sifrei* to expound and teach the basic principles of the Mishnah. R' Chiya compiled the *Tosefta* to explain the subject matter of the Mishnah. R' Hoshaya and Bar Kappara compiled *baraisos* to elucidate the text of the Mishnah. The sages of the Mishnah composed other works to expound the words of the Torah. [Another] R' Hoshaya, a disciple of R' Judah the Prince, wrote an exposition of *Genesis,* and R' Yishmael wrote a commentary on the Torah, from the beginning of *Exodus* through *Deuteronomy;* this is called *Mechilta.* R' Akiva also wrote a *Mechilta,* and other Sages compiled *midrashim.* All these works were composed before the Babylonian Talmud *(Rambam,* Introduction to *Yad).*

Two major classifications of works emerge according to *Rambam's* essay: (1) Commentaries on the Torah, and (2) the Mishnah.

The commentaries on the Torah may be further divided into two such categories: The first comprises the collections of *Aggadah* (nonlegal interpretations) based on various passages in Scripture. These include *Midrash Rabbah, Tanchuma,* and others. Some of the Sages devoted themselves entirely to this area and were subsequently called 'the Rabbis of the Aggadah' (see *Yerushalmi* to *Maasros* 1:2). We find an instance (ibid., *Yevamos* 4:2) in which these 'Rabbis of the Aggadah' are engaged in dispute with their counterparts, 'the Rabbis of the Halachah.' R' Avin the Levite, R' Tanchuma, R' Berachyah, R' Shimon HaChassid and R' Pinchas ben

Yair and many others were completely immersed in the study of *Aggadah* and *Midrash*, and are never mentioned in the purely legalistic dialectics.

The second subcategory contains the collections of legal interpretations of Scripture, such as *Mechilta, Sifra* and *Sifrei. Rambam* was referring to this category when he wrote that R' Yishmael and R' Akiva compiled *Mechilta* to elucidate the 'text of the Torah,' and that Rav compiled the *Sifra* and *Sifrei* to teach 'the principles of the Mishnah,' since these works explore Scripture for their halachic content.

The other major classification, the Mishnah (which includes the *Tosefta* and *baraisos* as well), is concerned mainly with expounding the laws, and only rarely does it cite verses from Scripture.[1] However, you will find the sources for the laws enumerated there in the *Mechilta, Sifra* and *Sifrei*.

For example, the Mishnah in *Arachin* (2:5) teaches: *There should never be less than six inspected lambs in the chamber of the lambs* (i.e., those used for the continual daily offerings). On the verse, *And it shall be in your keeping (Ex.* 12:6), *Mechilta* states: *The verse informs us that they would examine it ... From here [the Rabbis] said, 'There should never be less than six inspected lambs in the chamber of the lambs.'* Thus, we see clearly how works like the *Mechilta* identify the sources of the Mishnah's laws.

Regarding the difference between the mishnayos and the *baraisos, Tosafos* (*Bava Kamma* 94b, s.v. בימי) writes that the mishnayos predated Rabbi who then arranged them, whereas the *baraisos* were Rabbi's additions to the mishnayos, that R' Chiya subsequently compiled. However, the aforementioned passage in *Rambam* seems to suggest that the *baraisos* and *Tosefta* were commentaries on the Mishnah.

R' Shmuel Hanaggid writes in *Mevo HaTalmud:* 'Since Rabbi's composition of the Mishnah was quantitatively short and qualitatively great, containing not one unnecessary word — although it was clear and comprehensible to his brilliant mind, those who followed him were unable to fathom its depth; therefore, one of

---

1. In *Berachos* (5a) it says וְהַמִּצְוָה, *And the commandment (Ex. 24:12) — this is the Mishnah. Maharsha* explains that the Mishnah is called *commandment* because it addresses only the laws themselves. It is left to the *Gemara* to identify the source of the halachah in the Torah.

his disciples saw fit to write a book which would illuminate and elaborate on the words of his teacher. This was the *Tosefta,* which is essentially a commentary on the mishnayos.'

Perhaps *Tosafos* also intend this explanation and only disputed *Rambam* and *R' Shmuel Hanagid* on one point: that Rabbi himself added the commentary to the Mishnah, known as *Tosefta.*

The *Midrash (Koheles Rabbah* 2:8) which says: *The great mishnayos, such as the great Mishnah of R' Chiya and the great Mishnah of R' Oshaya*[2] *and the Mishnah of Bar Kappara,* is actually referring to their *baraisos,* yet the *Midrash* calls them 'great' mishnayos because they explained their subject matter at great length, unlike the concise mishnayos of Rabbi.

The question why one collection is called *baraisos* and the other *toseftos* has generated several opinions. Some maintain that Rabbi actually dictated the *Tosefta* to R' Chiya, in line with the expression: *If Rabbi did not teach it; from where did R' Chiya get it? (Eruvin* 92a, et al. The *baraisos,* on the other hand, were mishnayos taught outside of Rabbi's academy without his knowledge *(Halichos Olam,* Part I; see *Yavin Shemuah).*

The early authorities, however, explain that the *Tosefta* is an addition to the Mishnah and is therefore never introduced by the introduction תַּנְיָא, *it is taught,* or תָּנוּ רַבָּנָן, *the Rabbis taught,* but only by תְּנָא, *teach,* or תְּנָא עֲלָה, *teach on it,* which imply that what follows is an addition to the Mishnah *(Sefer Hakerisus).* [According to this opinion, the *Baraisa* is a separate work.]

Rambam seems to contend that both are commentaries on the Mishnah; however, the *Tosefta* seeks to explain the subject matter of the Mishnah, while the *baraisos* aim to illuminate the wording of the Mishnah.

Actually, all the compilations of the early Sages are included under the general title of *baraisos,* such as the Mishnah of R' Chiya and R' Oshaya, the *Masnisah* of Levi[3] and Bar Kappara, the Mishnah of R' Eliezer ben Yaakov, the *Mechilta* of R' Yishmael and R' Akiva, the *Osiyos* of R' Akiva, *Sifra* and *Sifrei.*

---

2. In *Yerushalmi (Kiddushin* 1:3), R' Oshaya is called 'Father of the Mishnah.'

3. On the *Gemara (Kesubos* 53b), *And so taught Levi in his masnisah, Rashi* writes: Levi compiled six orders of Baraisa, just as R' Chiya and R' Oshaya had done. (See also *Bava Metzia* (48a): *And Levi examined in his masnisah;* and *Rashi, Rashash* ad loc.)

The word itself, *baraisa,* means *external,* referring to the fact no material from these compilations entered Rabbi's composition of the Mishnah.

Mechilta is a commentary on the Book of *Exodus.* Its name derives from the Hebrew word for *measure.* The early authorities also used this word as a synonym for *sugya* (a Talmudic passage), writing *further in the mechilta,* rather than *further in the sugya.*

Sifra, on the Book of *Leviticus,* is also called *Toras Kohanim* (the Law of the Priests). The Sages referred to it as 'Lion' *(Berachos* 18b; see *Tos.* ad loc.) because it was the most difficult of those works. The *baraisa of Miluim* is a supplement to *Toras Kohanim* (see *Rashi* to *Lev.* 9:23).

Sifrei is composed of two volumes, one on *Numbers* and the other on *Deuteronomy.* It is also referred to as *the remaining books of the Academy,* since the volume on *Leviticus* was the most outstanding book.

The tractates known as מַסֶּכְתּוֹת קְטַנּוֹת, *the small tractates,* are *baraisos,* and are also called 'external tractates.'[4] The *Midrash (Koheles Rabbah* 5:8) says: *Even that which you might consider an addition to the original Law, such as the Tosafos of Beis Rabbi* (the *Tosefta* which Rabbi's disciples composed), *the Tosafos of R' Nassan (Avos d'Rabbi Nassan,* which is like a *Tosefta* to Tractate *Avos), or the Laws of Converts and Slaves, was also given to Moses on Sinai. And works such as the Laws of Tzitzis* (fringes), *Tefillin* (phylacteries) *and Mezuzos are authentic parts of the Torah.* The *Midrash* is indeed referring to the seven small tractates which were appended to the Talmud, namely: (1) *Geirim* (Converts), (2) *Kusim* (Cutheans), (3) *Avadim* (Slaves), (4) *Sefer Torah,* (5) *Tefillin,* (6) *Tzitzis,* and (7) *Mezuzah.*

Other small tractates not included in the Talmud are: (1) *Avos d'R' Nassan,* which R' Nassan composed while yet in Babylonia, before his immigration to the Holy Land. He was among the sages in the days of R' Shimon ben Gamliel, Rabbi's father *(Horayos* 13b)[5];

4. Because they were not included in the Six Orders. See *Ramban* to *Bava Metzia* 71b: *I found in an 'external'* [*tractate*], *in Tractate Kusim of the seven small tractates.*

5. Others reject the opinion that R' Nassan of Babylonia was its author. See *Maharatz Chayos,* citing *Rashi* to *Avos* 1:5, who states that there were two versions of *Avos d'Rabbi Nassan* — one from *Eretz Yisrael* and the other from France. Recently, both have been published.

(2) *Sofrim* (Scribes); (3) *Semachos* (Happy Occasions, a euphemism for Mourning); (4) *Kallah* (Bride); (5) *Derech Eretz* (Propriety); (6) *Eretz Yisrael;* (7) *Perek Hashalom* (Peace). Even though the expression *these are the words of the Amoraim* appears in some of the tractates, the greatest of the later commentators (see *Sedei Chemed, Klalei Haposkim* §2) have explained that certainly these tractates were compiled by *Tannaim,* but that subsequently some additions were made by *Amoraim,* just as the Rabbanan Savorai (see page 76) contributed to the Talmud that Ravina and R' Ashi had previously composed.

The *baraisos* can be recognized by the following introductory statements: תָּנוּ רַבָּנָן, *the Rabbis taught;* תָּנֵי חֲדָא, *one* [*sage*] *taught;* or תַּנְיָא אִידָךְ, *the other taught.* Use of the expression *the Rabbis taught* signifies that a particular *baraisa* is as well known as a mishnah (*Gufei Halachos* §87). *R' Sherira Gaon* writes, 'Those *baraisos* that R' Chiya and R' Oshaya wrote are superior to all others; the Sages took them and taught them, and the *Gemara* introduces them with the expression, *the Rabbis taught.* Nevertheless, there were other *baraisos* which the Sages taught, each according to what he received from his teacher... Yet these *baraisos* were not as well established as those of R' Chiya and R' Oshaya, and therefore they were never referred to as *the Rabbis taught,* but as תַּנְיָא, *it is taught,* or תַּנָא תּוּנָא, *our Tanna also taught like that.*[6]'

Wherever the *Gemara* introduces a *baraisa* with *The other teaches,* it is usually intended as a support for a previously stated *baraisa.*[7] Where the *Gemara* says תְּנַן, it is introducing a mishnah.[8]

It is well known that an anonymous mishnah reflects the opinion of R' Meir; an anonymous *Tosefta* the view of R' Nechemya; an anonymous *Sifra,* R' Yehudah; an anonymous *Sifrei,* R' Shimon[9] —

---

6. However, the later commentators cite from *Gittin* (73a) a *baraisa* which was introduced as *the Rabbis taught,* and which the *Gemara* declared unauthentic, having never been expounded in the study hall.

7. The exception to this rule is found in *Sotah* 15b, where the *Gemara's* intent is to introduce a conflicting *baraisa.*

8. However, on several occasions the *Gemara* prefaces a *baraisa* with תְּנַן. See *Horayos* 5a and *Kiddushin* 40a; also *Yad Malachi.*

9. *Chida* comments that the *Gemara* does not mean that R' Yehudah and R' Shimon composed the *Sifra* and *Sifrei,* respectively; rather, that the author of *Sifra* followed the view of R' Yehudah and so forth, just as an anonymous mishnah follows R'

and all of them according to R' Akiva. What they learned from R' Akiva, they taught *(Sanhedrin* 86a, *Rashi* ad loc.).

All the *Amoraim* were obligated to know the entire Mishnah, since it comprised the foundation of the Oral Law.[10] However, they were not required to know all the *baraisos.* Thus, we may find that the *Gemara* adduces proof from a *baraisa: It is taught in a baraisa like this Amora;* whereas if an *Amora* only reiterates a mishnah the *Gemara* interjects: *What is he telling us? It was already taught in a mishnah!* Nevertheless, the *Gemara* will occasionally provide support for an *Amora* from a mishnah. The rule is: If the law in the mishnah is explicitly stated, then they ask, *What is he telling us ...?* However, even an explicit *baraisa* may be offered as support for an *Amora's* position. But, if the law of a mishnah is only implied, then in that case they may say supportively, *We also learned it in a mishnah (Yad Malachi).*

Meir, even though Rabbi actually compiled the Mishnah. See *Sedei Chemed's* remarks *(Kelalei Haposkim* §2) on *Chida's comment.*

10. For even the teachings of R' Chiya and R' Oshaya are alluded to in the Mishnah. See *Kesubos* 69b.

Chapter Four
The Jerusalem Talmud

Authorship

R' Yochanan, a disciple of Rabbi, compiled the *Yerushalmi* (Jerusalem Talmud) in *Eretz Yisrael* (the Land of Israel) approximately three hundred years after the destruction of the Second Temple *(Rambam,* Introduction to *Yad).* However, *Ravad*[1] in *Seder Hakabbalah* writes: And in those days R' Yochanan — who received (the tradition) from R' Oshaya — was the *Rosh Yeshivah* (head of the academy) in the Holy Land, and he enjoyed a long life, serving in that capacity for eighty years.[2] He composed the *Yerushalmi* almost two hundred years after the destruction, and died in the year 4039 [279 c.e.].

R' Yochanan was known as Bar Nafcha (see *Rashi* to *Sanhedrin* 96a) and in *Yerushalmi* (to *Rosh Hashanah* 2:5) he is called *ben Hanafach* (son of the blacksmith). He was the brother-in-law and Talmudic adversary of Resh Lakish. He was the greatest of the *Amoraim* in the *Yerushalmi,* and was renowned for his love of Torah. Upon his passing it was said of him, (based on *Song of Songs* 8:7) 'Were any man to offer all the treasures of his home to entice R' Yochanan away from his love of the Torah, they would scorn him to the extreme' (*Yalkut Shimoni,* end of *Mishpatim).*

Initially, he was a student of Rabbi, and later studied in Caesarea under R' Oshaya, Rabbah, R' Yannai and R' Chanina. Afterwards,

---

1. The first of three early authorities referred to as such. His full name was R' Avraham ibn Daud.

2. Cf. *Iggeres R' Sherira Gaon,* which states that R' Yochanan died at the age of eighty in the year 4038 [278 c.e.].

he moved to Tiberias and founded a Talmudic academy, which attracted many great scholars and prospered until the *Yerushalmi* was completed.

That which was said above — that R' Yochanan composed and edited the *Yerushalmi* — does not mean that he completed it in its entirety, but only that he initiated and established its foundation. For a few generations after his passing the sages continued his holy work, completion finally coming some six generations after Rabbi. Similarly, when it is said that R' Ashi composed the Babylonian Talmud, the meaning is that he and Ravina only initiated the project, and that subsequently other *Amoraim* brought it to completion.

Orders and Tractates

It is apparent from the writings of the early authorities that they possessed a text of the *Yerushalmi* to *Kodashim;* for instance, *Ravad* comments in *Sefer HaKabbalah* that R' Yochanan composed the *Yerushalmi* in five orders. Also, *Rambam* (Introduction to *Mishnah Commentary*) writes that five complete orders[3] of the *Yerushalmi* have been found,[4] but a *Taharos* has never been found, neither in *Bavli* nor in *Yerushalmi*, except for the single tractate *Niddah.* In this vein *Rashi* (*Sukkah* 14a, s.v. משנ"ה) also writes that the tractates of *Taharos* have no existing *Gemara.* However, in their commentaries to *Taharos (Kelim,* 15:6), *R' Hai Gaon* and *Rash* both note that a 'Talmud' to *Kelim* was found in Rome.[5]

---

3. See *Ravad* to *Rambam, Hil. Bikkurim* 2:6, where he cites Tractate *Menachos* of the *Yerushalmi*, and also *Maggid Mishneh; Hil. Mechirah* 27:8, where he cites the *Yerushalmi* to Tractate *Arachin.*

4. Some want to infer from *Rambam's* using the terms *have been found* and *have not been found* that he was reporting only the number of orders extant in his day, indicating his belief that the *Yerushalmi* on all six orders had been composed, but that *Taharos* was missing. However, I heard several times from my great teacher, the *Chazon Ish* of sainted memory, that one may not make any inferences from the language of *Rambam's Mishnah Commentary,* since he originally wrote it in Arabic, and what we have is only a translation. Obviously, one cannot make such an inference from a translation.

5. *Kelim* is the first tractate in *Taharos.* However, it is possible that by 'talmud' they did not mean a *Gemara,* but only a commentary on the mishnayos. This interpretation seems more likely in light of what *R' Hai Gaon* himself comments there.

The *Yerushalmi* that we possess contains only four orders: (1) *Zeraim*,[6] (2) *Moed*, (3) *Nashim*, and (4) *Nezikin*. It also includes the first three chapters of *Niddah* and a fragment of the fourth. [*Tosafos* (*Niddah* 66a, s.v. 'ותבדוק הא') seem to imply that they had the seventh chapter of *Niddah* as well.] A few chapters are also missing from tractates *Shabbos* and *Makkos* in our *Yerushalmi*.

Style

Many proper names which in the Babylonian Talmud end with the letter א, such as חִיָּיא, עֲקִיבָא, in the majority of cases end with the letter ה in *Yerushalmi*, חִיָּיה, עֲקִיבָה. Where א begins a name in *Bavli* (אוֹשַׁעְיָא), you will find its counterpart in *Yerushalmi* beginning with ה (הוֹשַׁעְיָא). Similarly, יְהוּדָה in the *Bavli* reads יוּדָא in *Yerushalmi*, and the letters ע ,ח, ה, א are interchangeable in the latter, such as עִוְיָא — חִיוְיָא, and אֵיכָן — הֵיכָן. The later commentators note that throughout the years the language of the *Bavli* has remained intact — grammatically precise, following the rules of tense, gender and number — whereas many mistakes and imperfections in these areas have crept into the *Yerushalmi* over the years.

One stylistic trait of the *Yerushalmi* is to run together two adjacent words, so that an א or ה at the end of the first word or beginning of the second is completely swallowed up. Thus, *Abba Mari* becomes *Avmari*, *Rav Asi* turns into *Ravsi*, and *Rav Ami* to *Ravmi*. The *Gemara* notes: *This Tanna is a Jerusalemite, who uses a contracted form of expression (Bava Kamma* 6b). Actually, we find many instances of contractions in *Bavli* as well — *Rami* for *Rav Ami*, *Ravin* for *Rav Avin*, *Ravina* for *Rav Avina* and *Rafram* for *Rav Ephraim*, among others.

In general, the language of the *Yerushalmi* is peculiar[7]

---

6. In its entirety. In *Zeraim* of the Babylonian Talmud, however, there is *Gemara* only on Tractate *Berachos*.

7. It appears, however, that *Yerushalmi* was intentionally written in enigmas. This is evident from Tractate *Demai* of the *Yerushalmi* (7:6): *Whoever has produce and wishes to tithe it, should twice separate nine parts from one hundred, and then another one part, totaling ten parts for maaser rishon* (the first tithe) *and nine parts for maaser sheini* (the second tithe). *But say (more directly), 'Take nineteen parts'? R' Ze'ira said: It is the way of the Sages to speak in riddles.*

Thus, we see clearly that the Sages of *Yerushalmi* would intentionally express themselves enigmatically. Perhaps they were motivated by the desire to instill a love

(Introduction to *Darkei HaMishnah*). *Rashi* (*Sotah* 49b) writes: The Syrian language is similar to Aramaic. I say that it is the language of the *Yerushalmi* ...

---

of Torah in the hearts of its students, inasmuch as one values his achievements in proportion to the effort expended in attaining them.

In the beginning of Tractate *Maaser Sheini*, for example, it is taught that a man asked his friend, 'What did you eat today?' and the other replied, 'Manna' — hinting that he ate for free that day, just as the manna itself cost nothing. When he wanted to say that his food was inexpensive, he would answer that he ate a firstborn animal, since it was inexpensive. The Rabbis were obviously teaching that one should weigh his every word, and speak only what is absolutely necessary. [See also *Eruvin* (53b), where they speak enigmatically.]

Every man should be careful not to overburden his listeners, and certainly — when speaking words of Torah — he should choose the correct occasion, place, and length of time to speak, and then do so in a manner befitting himself and his audience. Once, a sage spoke for a very long time on a particular subject. When asked why he did so, the sage explained that he wanted the simple-minded people to understand. They retorted that while the simple ones are comprehending, the intelligent people are becoming disgruntled. However, when one speaks cleverly in riddles and allusions his expression is perforce constrained (*Meiri* to *Avos* 1:1 on עשו סייג לתורה).

I have heard it pointed out that *Rambam* does not include the rule that one should instruct his students in a concise manner in *Hilchos Talmud Torah*, as one might expect, but rather in *Hilchos Deos* — the Laws of Ethics or Moral Dispositions — since this rule more closely pertains to ethical conduct than to the science of instruction.

Chapter Five
The Babylonian Talmud and the Amoraim

Rav and Shmuel

Rav and Shmuel were students of Rabbi. They emigrated to Babylonia and became heads of renowned Talmudic academies there — Shmuel in Nehardea and Rav in Sura.

Rav's real name was Abba *(Aruch* quoting *R' Sherira Gaon* and *R' Hai Gaon),* and he was also called Abba Aricha.[1] *Rashi* writes that Shmuel called him *Abba* [literally, 'father'] because the name itself suggests its bearer's importance. However, *Rashi* does not mean that Rav's name was not actually Abba; rather, since Abba was known to all as Rav, Shmuel's use of the name Abba was intended as an acknowledgment of Rav's greatness. Indeed, Rav is mentioned three times in *baraisos* as R' Abba.

Rav taught R' Chiya the hidden subjects of the Torah and learned from R' Chiya its revealed parts — the Mishnah and *Gemara (Kanfei Yonah).* He was R' Chiya's nephew. Rav's father was Aivo ben Abba bar Acha Karsela from Kafri *(Sanhedrin* 5a). He was called Rav (Master), the Babylonian equivalent of Rabbi in Eretz Yisrael. Since he was the *Rosh Yeshivah* in Babylon, he was known simply as Rav, just as R' Judah the Prince was called Rabbi in the Holy Land. Similarly, the *Amoraim* in Babylon received the title *Rav* (e.g., Rav Yosef and Rav Chama), while their counterparts in Eretz Yisrael were honored with the appellation רַבִּי, *Rabbi,* before their names.

1. Just as R' Eliezer was called Hagadol, 'the Great' [see page 36], so was Rav called Abba Aricha, 'the Great.' However, see *Chullin* 137b and *Rashi* ad loc., that Aricha means *tall one,* and refers to his height.

Rav, in Aramaic, means *master* or *minister*, as in *Rav Tabachim*, the minister appointed over the (king's) executioners (*II Kings* 25:8, see *Metzudas David* ad loc.).

Rav was considered a *Tanna* and could therefore dispute other *Tannaim*, since he was a contemporary and friend of Rabbi's two sons, R' Gamliel and R' Shimon, who were themselves *Tannaim*. *R' Hai Gaon* adduces as further proof the fact that Rav is cited three times in the *Baraisa*.

It was said of Rav that he never spoke an idle word his entire life (*Rambam, Hil. Deos* 2:4), and that he never walked four cubits without being occupied in the study of Torah or without wearing *tzitzis* and *tefillin* (*Rambam, Hil. Tefillin* 4:25).

The degree to which Rav would exert and dedicate himself to ascertain full knowledge of a law is related by the *Gemara* (*Sanhedrin* 5b). Rav lived with a shepherd for eighteen months in order to learn the difference between a permanent blemish and a temporary one [as regards the laws of offerings]. Thus, he was willing to degrade himself and to live at length among common people for the sake of a small detail of halachah, something that even an average person — lacking Rav's enormous stature — would not do. Because of his love for the Torah, however, Rav was willing to undergo any experience (*Chofetz Chaim* in *Toras Habayis*).

Rav composed the prayers in the Rosh Hashanah *Mussaf* service that precede and follow the three sets of Scriptural verses on the themes of God's Kingship, Remembrance and the Shofar. The Sages refer to this liturgy as תְּקִיעֲתָא דְרַב (lit., *the shofar blowing of Rav*) (*Yerushalmi* to *Rosh Hashanah* 1:3; see *Ramban* to *Deut.* 33:5).

Rav's great colleague, Shmuel, was a *Kohen*. He was called by three sobriquets: (1) *Shakud*, because he toiled *conscientiously* and *arduously* to learn the Torah in accordance with the Halachah; (2) *Aryoch*, which *Rashi* (*Menachos* 38b) derives from אַרְיֵה, and defines as *king*, as in גּוּר אַרְיֵה יְהוּדָה, *like a young lion is Judah* (*Gen.* 49:9), where the meaning is *king*. Shmuel was called Aryoch because the halachah conforms with his opinion in civil matters (*Bechoros* 49b), as in his ruling that דִּינָא דְמַלְכוּתָא דִּינָא, *the law of the government is binding according to Jewish law*; (3) *Shavor Malka*, because of his friendship with the Persian king of that name.

He was well versed in all the sciences, especially in astronomy and medicine, and served as Rabbi's personal physician. Rabbi desired to ordain him, but did not succeed in doing so. Shmuel told him that he had seen the *Book of Adam,* in which was stated that Shmuel Yarchinai shall be called a sage, but not a Rabbi *(Bava Metzia* 85b). Shmuel was called Mar Shmuel, and his father was Abba bar Abba the *Kohen.*

Rav, Shmuel, and R' Yochanan are called *verses of the Scripture* in the *Gemara (Avodah Zarah* 40a). *Rashi* (ad loc.) explains that they were such outstanding scholars that one could rely on them as upon Scripture itself.

During the lifetime of Rav, R' Yochanan used to address him thus in his letters: 'Greetings to our Master in Babylon!' After Rav's death R' Yochanan would address Shmuel: 'Greetings to our colleague in Babylon!' Shmuel said to himself: 'Is there nothing in which I am his master?' (i.e., 'Isn't there any subject in which I am more expert than he?'). He then sent R' Yochanan the calculations for the intercalations of months for sixty years. [Unimpressed,] R' Yochanan remarked, 'He knows mere calculations.' So Shmuel wrote out and sent R' Yochanan thirteen camel-loads of questions concerning doubtful cases of *treifa.* Said R' Yochanan, 'I have a master in Babylon. I must go and see him' *(Chullin* 95b, *Rashi* ad loc.; see ch. 1 regarding R' Elazar Chisma).

In any legal dispute between Rav and Shmuel the halachah follows Shmuel in civil matters and Rav in ritual law. A mnemonic for this is: *Aryoch, king of Ellasar* [אֶלָּסָר] *(Gen.* 14:1) — which would mean, *Aryoch* (or Shmuel, as we have discussed) is *king,* but אֶלָּסָר, or אַל אִיסוּר, *not prohibitions* — i.e., not regarding ritual law, since in this area the law conforms with Rav's opinion. Where the dispute basically concerns a civil matter, but has ramifications in the area of ritual law, the halachah is nonetheless like Shmuel. Likewise, when the controversy centers around ritual law, but has some bearing on civil matters, the ruling follows Rav *(Yad Malachi).*

Rav and Shmuel composed a precious gem in Babylon — the *Havdalah* prayer entitled וַתּוֹדִיעֵנוּ, *You made known to us,* which is recited when a festival falls on Saturday night *(Berachos* 33b).[2]

❦ ❦ ❦

2. *Maharsha* explains that this prayer was not composed previously by the Sages in *Eretz Yisrael* because the festivals rarely fall on Saturday night there. However, in Babylonia, where they observed a second day of the festival as required in the

The students of Rav and Shmuel were: R' Huna, R' Yehudah bar Yechezkel — who composed the blessing on sanctifying the new moon *(Sanhedrin* 42a; see *Sefer Habris* vol. I, 4:2) — and R' Nachman bar Yaakov *(Tos.* to *Gittin* 31b), who was the son-in-law of the *Resh Galusa* (head of the nation in exile). He and his peers established the *shevuos heses,* an oath imposed upon one who has been sued for a debt and entirely denies the claim.[3]

R' Yochanan's disciples included: Rabbah bar bar Channah,[4] R' Ami, R' Assi, R' Dimi, R' Avin, R' Chiya bar Abba,[5] and R' Abahu. *Yerushalmi* (*Shabbos* 1:1) relates that once R' Abahu went down to Tiberias, where R' Yochanan's students spotted him, his face beaming. The students reported to R' Yochanan that R' Abahu must have found a precious stone or the like, for his glowing countenance bespoke an inner delight. R' Yochanan suggested that, on the contrary, perhaps R' Abahu had just heard a new Torah teaching. They sought out R' Abahu and asked him what new teaching he had heard. 'An ancient *tosefta,*' he replied. Of him they proclaimed: *The wisdom of a man causes his countenance to shine (Eccl.* 8:1).

R' Abahu established the order of shofar blowing on Rosh Hashanah *(Rosh Hashanah* 34a).

❦ ❦ ❦

The disciples of R' Huna and R' Yehudah included Rabbah bar Nachmani and R' Yosef bar Chiya. R' Sheshes was the principal disciple of R' Huna, and is called *a man hard as iron (Menachos* 95b), which means that he was sharp as a blade of iron to carve out the correct halachah.

Diaspora, one of those days often coincided with the departure of the Sabbath. The language of the prayer itself indicates that it was composed in the Diaspora, for the phrase, חַגֵּי נְדָבָה, *free-willed festive offerings,* refers to the second day of the festival, which is like a free-will offering.

3. See *Toras Chaim* to *Shevuos* 48 regarding the dispute between *Rashi* and *Tosafos.*

4. *Shaar HaMelech* explains that since his father was also called Rabbah (see *Sanhedrin* 5a, *Tos.* ad loc.), his contemporaries did not want to call him Rabbah bar Rabbah — thus, the name Rabbah bar bar Channah. Once this was done, his brother became known as R' Shmuel bar bar Channah *(Shabbos* 29a). Rabba bar Channah, their father, was the nephew of Rav.

5. He would review what he had learned every thirty days before R' Yochanan, his teacher *(Berachos* 38b).

❦ ❦ ❦

In legal disputes between R' Sheshes and R' Nachman, the halachah follows R' Sheshes' opinion in ritual law and R' Nachman's in civil matters *(Rosh* to *Sukkah* 44b, quoting *Teshuvas Hageonim).* However, even though Shmuel takes precedence over Rav in civil law, as discussed above, and R' Nachman over R' Sheshes — nevertheless, in a dispute between Rav and R' Nachman regarding civil matters the halachah follows Rav *(Yad Malachi).*

Rashi[6] explains that we follow R' Nachman's decisions in civil law because he was the son-in-law of the *nasi,* and frequented the courts where civil cases were decided. Thus, he was able to observe how the law was actually interpreted. *Rosh* (to *Bava Kamma* 37b) similarly explains that the halachah follows Rav in ritual law and Shmuel in civil matters because each had much experience deciding cases in his respective field of expertise.

In controversies between Rabbah and R' Yosef the law always concurs with Rabbah's opinion, except in three cases, when we follow R' Yosef's view (see page 96).

Abaye and Rava

The greatest disciples of Rabbah and R' Yosef were Abaye and Rava, who also studied under R' Nachman.

Abaye was a *Kohen,* and his father was Kylil *(Zevachim* 118b). Abaye was named Nachmani after his grandfather, who was also Rabbah's father. He was Rabbah's nephew and disciple. The early authorities *(Aruch; Rashi)* explain that although Abaye's real name was Nachmani, Rabbah did not want to call him so, since that was Rabbah's father's name as well. He therefore substituted Abaye, the Aramaic term of *my father* — simiiar to the Hebrew אָבִי, *avi* — and the name stuck. Others, however, explain that Abaye was his real name, but since Rabbah had raised him as a son and taught him Torah, he called the youth Nachmani after his own father[7] (see *Rashi* to *Gittin* 34b).

---

6. Though this statement has been attributed to *Rashi,* in our editions we find it only in *Rashbam (Bava Basra* 65a).

7. See *Seder Hadoros,* who quotes *Be'er Sheva* that *Rashi* (end of *Horayos)* explains that *Nachmani* was applied to Abaye pejoratively, in the sense of *you are still the student of R' Nachman.* However, *Be'er Sheva* opines that this was not written by *Rashi,* and is an erroneous addition of some student.

Abaye's father died before his birth, and his mother died immediately thereafter. Abaye's name (אַבַּיֵי) is an acronym formed by the first letters in the verse *(Hoshea* 14:4), אֲשֶׁר בְּךָ יְרֻחַם יָתוֹם, *only by You will the orphan be pitied.*

The *Gemara* tells us that when Abaye says, *My mother told me,* he is referring to his nursemaid.

Rava was the son of R' Yosef bar Chama *(Nedarim* 53a). So intensely did he study the Torah that once while learning he inadvertently put his fingers under his feet and ground them down, so that they spurted blood and he did not even notice *(Shabbos* 88a, *Rashi* ad loc.).

In any legal dispute between early and later *Amoraim,* the halachah is decided in favor of the later authority, except in the case of a disciple who disputes his teacher in the locality of the latter. However, from the time of Abaye and Rava and onward the halachah always follows the later authority — even a disciple who disagrees with his teacher to his face, and even a later *Amora* who disputes a predecessor who lived before Abaye and Rava. These rules, however, are not universally accepted.

Any controversy between Abaye and Rava is always decided according to Rava's opinion — with six exceptions, when the halachah follows Abaye. יַע״ל קְגַ״ם is the mnemonic acronym used by the *Gemara* to note the six exceptions. The first letter, י, stands for יֵאוּשׁ, *abandonment* of a lost article *(Bava Metzia* 21b); ע for עֵד זוֹמֵם, *a plotting witness* whose disqualification is retroactive *(Sanhedrin* 27a); ל for לֶחִי, *a pole* not purposely inserted for the sake of carrying in a certain area on the Sabbath[8] *(Eruvin* 15a); ק for קִידוּשִׁין, *the first stage of marriage* — whether one that cannot result in actual cohabitation takes effect or not *(Kiddushin* 51a); ג for גִילוּי, *revealing* one's attitude indirectly in regard to a *get* [bill of divorce] *(Gittin* 34a); and מ for מוּמָר, *an apostate* who eats unkosher meat to show his contempt for the law *(Sanhedrin* 27a).

The Talmud overflows with the words of Abaye and Rava. I have heard that there are no four consecutive folios of the entire

---

8. This follows *Rashi's* view. *Rabbeinu Tam* in *Tosafos* maintains that the *lamed* stands for לֵידָה, *childbirth,* and refers to the view that the days following birth are not included in the count for *zivah* (a type of ritual uncleanness; see *Lev.* 15:25) if there is no flow of blood. The sons of Narvona offer yet another possibility: The *lamed* stands for לֹא אֶפְשָׁר וְלֹא קָמְכַוֵּין, a topic discussed in *Pesachim* 25b.

Babylonian Talmud that do not mention either Abaye or Rava. (But this is not precise.) The topical passages of the *Gemara* and the halachic debates are termed *the disputes between Abaye and Rava.*

Hillel served as *nasi* during the era of Abaye and Rava.[9] He, his court, and the sages of that time established for us — based on the tradition they received from their predecessors — an accurate and revised method of calculating the first day of each month and, hence, the dates of all the festivals *(Sefer Yochasin,* end of §5). [This is not to say that they invented this science of fixing the calendar; rather, it had previously been taught — allusively — in a *baraisa (Rosh Hashanah* 20b, see *Rashi* ad loc.)] *Rambam* writes: R' Hillel the *Nasi* ... established the method of fixing the calendar, which involves determining the day to sanctify the new month, and determined which years should be expanded by an additional month, until such time as Elijah will come and we shall once again sanctify the new month upon receiving testimony in the great and holy Sanhedrin from witnesses who actually saw the new moon.[10] For Hillel foresaw that just as the decline of ordained, expert judges caused the cancellation of קְנָסוֹת, *monetary penalties,* so too would the holy festivals be abandoned for lack of certainty as to their specific dates of observance. Thus, he formulated the method of fixing the calendar until the advent of Elijah *(Sefer Hamitzvos,* Positive Commandment 153; see also *Rambam's* opinion ibid.).

Ravina and R' Ashi

Among Rava's greatest disciples were Ravina and R' Ashi[11] *(Rambam,* Introduction to *Yad).* However, they were two generations apart; the intervening generation of *Amoraim* included

---

9. He was the last *nasi* named Hillel. See page 87 for his relationship to Hillel the Elder.

10. See *Sofrim* 19:9, that they would make a special blessing when they were worthy of performing the commandment of sanctifying the new month based on the testimony of eyewitnesses.

11. Regarding the *Gemara (Kiddushin* 72b) which states: *When Rava died, R' Ashi was born, Rambam's* text reads: *Before Rava died, R' Ashi was born (*according to *Halichos Olam). Sefer Kinus Sofrim* (there and in his glosses to *Niddah* 51a) proves that *Rashi* follows *Rambam's* view. *Tosafos* (*Chullin* 2b, s.v. אנא), however, maintain that Abaye and Rava lived long before R' Ashi.

R' Pappa; R' Huna, the son of R' Yehoshua, R' Zevid, and others who were also students of Abaye and Rava.

Since the days of R' Judah the Prince, never were Torah scholarship and wealth found in one individual — until R' Ashi. God arranged that he find favor in the eyes of the Persian king. R' Ashi gathered all the Jewish sages from throughout the world to sit together and elucidate the Mishnah, a monumental effort which produced the Babylonian Talmud with the approbation of all the wise men of his generation *(Rambam* ibid.). R' Ashi was exceptionally humble, and recognized the enormous responsibility of one who decides the law. Thus, whenever a *treifa* (an animal afflicted with an internal wound or disease) was submitted to him for inspection, he sent for all the slaughterers of Masa Mechasya who were experts in these laws, saying, *let each of them carry off a chip from the beam* (i.e., should we err, let the punishment be divided among us, and thereby be lightened) *(Sanhedrin* 7b). See *Bava Basra* (3b) regarding R' Ashi's conduct during the construction of a synagogue in Masa Mechasya.

R' Ashi compiled the Babylonian Talmud in the land of Shinar (Babylon) approximately one hundred years after R' Yochanan completed the Jerusalem Talmud. Afterwards, many tragedies befell the people, and the sages were forced to disperse all over the world. As intellectual capacity waned, they began to commit the Talmud to writing *(R' Moshe of Coucy* in his introduction to *Semag).*

Our teachers have revealed that words or phrases in the *Gemara* that appear extraneous or imprecise actually contain deep and hidden meanings. For example, we are told in *Bava Kamma* (39b): *The bull of a deaf-mute, a mentally deranged person or a minor — R' Yaakov pays half-damages.* The *Gemara* proceeds to ask why R' Yaakov must pay, and answers that the text must be amended to read: *R' Yaakov says: He (the perpetrator) pays half the damages.* However, the original expression itself, *R' Yaakov pays,* actually contains a concealed meaning. There are many other instances of this (see *Sefer Habris* vol. I, ch. 8, quoting the *Gaon, R' Yoseph Irgas,* of blessed memory).

R' Ashi and Ravina concluded the era of הוֹרָאָה, *authoritative Talmudic teaching.*[12] An allusion to this is the verse, *When I*

12. [That is, the foundations of halachic exegesis were completed during the Talmudic era; from that time onward, future sages could not dispute the Talmud,

entered the Sanctuary of God, *then I understood their end (Psalms* 73:17). Samuel saw this in the *Book of Adam (Bava Metzia* 86a). *Rashi* (ad loc.) explains: R' Ashi and Ravina concluded the era of *Amoraim.* Before them the Talmud had never been organized. Rather, questions pertaining to the Mishnah had been posed in the academies, or the complexities of real-life situations had inspired questions on civil or ritual law, and the *Amoraim* would respond, each rendering his own reasoned opinion. R' Ashi and Ravina arranged these under the headings of the appropriate mishnayos, according to the order of the tractates. They and their colleagues asked questions on the Mishnah and gave the appropriate answers, and then made them part of the *Gemara,* introducing the questions with suitable heading such as אֵיתִיבֵיה, *He asked against him,* מֵיתִיב, *they asked,* and the like, along with their answers. Neither the questions and answers left over from the earlier *Amoraim,* nor those from the contemporary sages, had ever been included in the *Gemara* according to the order of tractates and mishnayos that Rabbi established, until R' Ashi and Ravina did so. A sign thereof is the verse *(Psalms* 73:17), *When I entered the Sanctuary of God ...* מִקְדְשֵׁי, *sanctuary,* alludes to R' Ashi (אַשִׁי), and אָבִינָה, *I understood,* refers to Ravina (רָבִינָא). The phrase, *their end,* signifies the end of *authoritative Talmudic* teaching.

It is written that *R' Sherira Gaon* said that אָבִינָה refers to a later *Amora* named Ravina, who was the son of R' Huna from Sura and served as *Rosh Yeshivah* in Sura after Rabba Tosfaah. The earlier Ravina, the contemporary of R' Ashi, was his mother's brother. The later Ravina was a disciple of Mereimar, and it was he who finalized the Talmud. According to this opinion, then, the pair of Ravina and R' Ashi, with regard to the *Gemara,* parallels the pair of R' Nassan and Rabbi, regarding the *Mishnah;* i.e., there, too, R' Nassan preceded Rabbi by one generation (see page 48).

R' Ashi wrote two drafts of the Talmud — one lengthy and the other more concise, just as any author edits and revises his manuscript *(Halichos Olam). Rashbam* cites *R' Hai Gaon* and *R' Chananel* that R' Ashi labored thirty years on the first edition, and another thirty on the second version.

---

but would deal with questions and problems by interpreting the principles set forth in the Talmud.]

Mar bar R' Ashi

Mar bar R' Ashi received the tradition from his father, R' Ashi *(Chullin* 76b; *Eruvin* 105b; Rambam, Introduction to *Yad)* and from Ravina. The *Rishonim* note that the halachah follows his opinion throughout the Talmud, with the exceptions of the laws of transferring an oath *(Shevuos* 41a), a document confessing a debt *(Sanhedrin* 29b), and some include the shade of whiteness of an animal's tendons necessary to be considered part of the juncture of the tendons *(Chullin* 76b). The mnemonic is הָפַךְ לָבָן, *turned white.* Others hold the opposite view, that *only* in these cases does the halachah follow him. He used to sign his correspondence *Tavyumi* *(Bava Basra* 12b; see *Maharsha* there for various explanations of the name). Rabba Tosfaah[13] lived in his generation, which was the last of the *Amoraim.*

Summary

In conclusion, we shall briefly review the order of the Torah's transmission from Sinai through the era of the Amoraim:

1. Moses, our Teacher, who received the entire Torah from the Almighty on Sinai in the presence of the entire Jewish nation
2. Joshua
3. The Elders
4. The Prophets — one following the other
5. Shimon the Tzaddik, who was a member of the Great Assembly
6. Antigonus
7. Yose ben Yoezer and Yose ben Yochanan
8. Yehoshua ben Perachyah and Nitai of Arbel
9. Yehudah ben Tabai and Shimon ben Shatach
10. Shemayah and Avtalyon
11. Shammai and Hillel
12. R' Shimon, from his father Hillel
13. his son R' Gamliel the Elder

---

13. He was called *Tosfaah* because he was well versed in the *Tosefta.* Others suggest that he was called after his place of origin (R' *Shlomo ben Hayasom* in his commentary to *Moed Katan* 4a).

14. his son R' Shimon
15. his son R' Gamliel
16. his son R' Shimon
17. his son R' Judah the Prince
18. Rav and Shmuel
19. R' Huna and R' Yehudah
20. Rabbah and R' Yosef
21. Rava
22. R' Ashi and Ravina
23. Mar bar R' Ashi

Chapter Six
Rabbanan Savorai and Geonim

Rabbanan Savorai

Even though Ravina and R' Ashi concluded the era of authoritative Talmudic teaching, the Talmud was not actually completed in their lifetimes (see page 62). There were those who pondered the teachings of the *Amoraim* to explain and interpret them, and clarify all the obscurities. They were called *Rabbanan Savorai.* Among them were R' Rechumi, Rabbah Yose, and R' Acha from the house of Chatim. The expositions of some, such as R' Eina and R' Simuna, were actually incorporated into the *Gemara (R' Sherira Gaon).*

Since they did not add to or delete from the content of the *Gemara,* but supplied only explanations and interpretations, they were called *Rabbanan Savorai* (the Ponderers). *Shalsheles HaKabbalah* writes that during the period in which they lived extraordinary sufferings befell the people, and the scholars were unable to study in tranquility. Therefore, they sought to understand the mishnayos through logical argument [סְבָרָא], and hence were called *Rabbanan Savorai.* They were lavishly praised for their purity and for their ability to retain all that they learned[1] *(Shem Hagedolim* quoting *Sefer Hakaneh).*

---

1. Apparently, the intent is that since they understood everything and forgot nothing, they were called *Rabbanan Savorai* (from סבר, *understand).*

R' Sherira Gaon writes that he received a tradition that the section of Tractate *Kiddushin* from the beginning until 3b was inserted by the *Rabbanan Savorai.*

Rambam (*Zavim* 4:6) notes that the definition drawn by the *Gemara (Niddah 4b)* from Scripture for the word מְדָף (an object that is impure to a minor degree) was not originally part of the text, but was actually a marginal note citing the explanation of the *Savoraim,* which a later transcriber mistakenly included in the text. Likewise, the *Geonim* (see below), who followed the *Savoraim,* added to the *Gemara. Ritva* notes that the passage in *Bava Metzia* (3a) beginning; *According to the views of both the Sages and R' Yose, there in the case of the shopkeeper and his credit book ...* was a later addition of Mar Yehudai Gaon. Also in *Bava Metzia* (see *Shitah Mekubetzes* ibid. 15b) the passage beginning, *Both according to Rav ... and ... Shmuel ... how does he go down to the field ...* was inserted into the original text by R' Yehudai Gaon. The composition of the Mishnah itself, which was initiated by R' Judah the Prince, was continued and eventually completed by his students. Proof of this may be adduced from the mishnah in *Sotah* (49a): *After Rabbi's death, humility and fear of sin disappeared.* Certainly, only Rabbi's disciples could have written that. On the *Gemara (Bava Metzia* 86a) *Rabbi and R' Nassan finalized the Mishnah, Rashi* (ad loc.) comments that they collected what was taught before them and arranged the tractates; their successors added only a little.

The first generation of *Rabbanan Savorai* were the students of Mar bar R' Ashi and Rabbah Tosfaah, and included R' Sama the son of Rava (who is mentioned in *Kesubos* 33b); R' Sama, the son of R' Yehudai; R' Rechumi; R' Shmuel, the son of R' Avuha (mentioned in *Chullin* 49b); Ravina bar Umtzia; Rav Huna the *Resh Galusa* (Head of the Jews in Exile); R' Achai, the son of Rabbah bar Avuha; R' Tachna, and Mar Zutra, the sons of Chinenah; and R' Yose was the last of that generation.

The second generation, disciples of the first, included R' Eina and R' Simuna.

The third generation, their disciples: R' Ravai Merov (mentioned in *Sanhedrin* 43a, according to *R' Chananel's* version).

The fourth and final generation of *Rabbanan Savorai* consisted of R' Giza, R' Huna and R' Dimi Sorgo.

The Geonim

The generations of *Geonim* followed the era of the *Rabbanan Savorai. Meiri* (Introduction to *Avos)* describes the state of the yeshivos during the period of the *Geonim:*

The academies were large and venerable institutions with many students who devoted themselves exclusively to Torah study. Certainly, the heads of these yeshivos and those who were ordained *Geonim* never stepped foot out of the 'tent of Torah,' but studied day and night and knew the entire Talmud by heart, or at least nearly all of it. They were as familiar and facile with the words of the Torah and Talmud as with those in the *Shema.* For that reason they never felt the need to write extensively, since they had the explanations for every aspect of the Torah at their fingertips, and so to record them would be the equivalent of a contemporary scholar writing down a simple translation of the text. Thus, they composed only a small quantity of commentary and legal decisions, and even that was not written for themselves, but only for their sons and relatives who requested brief treatises on specific areas of ritual and civil law. We have received an unimpeachable tradition that R' Acha of blessed memory had a son who did not want to expend effort in Torah study. Hence, R' Acha wrote *Sefer HaSheiltos* for him, so that when he reviewed the Torah-reading of each Sabbath he would be able to learn the pertinent laws of the Talmud.

We also know that Rabbeinu Saadyah, of blessed memory, wrote *Sefer Hapikadon* for someone who had just been appointed a judge in his town, a place where many merchants lived. Since they often gave items to each other for safekeeping, they were constantly disputing the laws and thus quarreled often. The new judge was sometimes unsure of the law, and so R' Saadyah tried to clarify for him the general laws of the subject. Similarly, most of the written works of the *Geonim* were not undertaken to benefit the public, for there was really no such need, since the yeshivos were so well established that *the land was filled with the knowledge of God (Isaiah* 11:9). Among the people were those who knew three of the Six Orders (Moed, Nashim and Nezikin), and they were called sages *(chachamim).* Those who knew four orders (the previous three, as well as *Kodashim)* were referred to as *rav;* and those who knew all six orders were worthy to be called גָּאוֹן, *gaon*, a title that by its numerical value alludes to the sixty tractates of the Talmud.[2] However, only those who were ordained by another *Gaon* with the approval of the yeshivah were actually called *Geonim*. The heads of the yeshivos were *Geonim* who knew the entire Talmud by heart, and when they taught in their yeshivos their words issued forth in rapid succession with no trace of hesitation. When the *Rosh Yeshivah* passed away, they chose as his successor the one most worthy to be a *Gaon*, the most knowledgeable among them, and the one who was most likely to succeed in his endeavors.

All the sages who, after the compilation of the Talmud, studied it deeply and became famous for their wisdom are called *Geonim*. All these *Geonim*, who flourished in *Eretz Yisrael*, in Shinar (Babylon), Spain and France, taught the method of the Talmud, elucidated its obscurities, and expounded its subject matter, for its method is exceedingly profound. Furthermore, the work is a mixture of Aramaic with other languages, since Aramaic was the vernacular of the Babylonian Jews at the time the Talmud was compiled. In other countries, however, as well as in Babylon during the era of the *Geonim*, no one — unless he had been taught it specifically — understood that language. Many requests were made to the sages of the day by the residents of each city to clarify difficulties in the Talmud, and the *Geonim* responded according to their ability. Those who had submitted the questions collected the responsa, which they subsequently made into books for study; these were the *Teshuvos HaGeonim*. The *Geonim* of each generation also composed commentaries on the Talmud. Some of them explained specific laws; others, particular chapters that presented difficulties to their contemporaries; still others expounded complete tractates and orders of the Talmud. They also compiled legal decisions pertaining to the ritual and penal law that was relevant to the times, so that anyone unable to penetrate the depths of the Talmud might know them. And this is the heavenly endeavor in which the *Geonim* were engaged from the day the Talmud was completed *(Rambam, Introduction to Yad)*.

---

2. Some have challenged this, claiming that there are actually sixty-three tractates. Even if the three *Bavas* are counted as one, the total is still sixty-one. However, see page 52, that some other tractates are also counted as one, and so according to all opinions the total number is sixty.

R' Yosef (Ri) Migash writes in his *Responsa* (§14) that an authority who decides the law on the basis of the responsa of the *Geonim* is more reliable than one who reaches his conclusions through his own study of the Talmudic sources. The former, even though he does not analyze the textual sources himself, is nevertheless acting upon the teaching of a great and expert court which itself established the law, while the latter — who relies on his own analysis — should be prevented from doing so, for in our times no one is capable of ascertaining the essential wisdom of the Talmud on his own without consulting the opinion of the *Geonim*.

However, the *Rishonim* (who followed the *Geonim)* were divided as to whether the decisions of the *Geonim* should be considered on par with those of the Talmud, in which case subsequent authorities would be incapable of contradicting them (see *Baal Hamaor to Sanhedrin* 32a).

Ramban writes in regard to certain liturgical customs of Rosh Hashanah: Since the *Geonim* attest that this was always their custom, we must therefore accept their testimony. For the *Geonim* received the tradition from the *Rabbanan Savorai,* and the latter from the *Amoraim,* who sat in the yeshivah of Rav Ashi and prayed in his synagogue *(Milchamos Hashem,* end of *Rosh Hashanah,* quoted by *Rosh* ibid.).

The Generations of Geonim

The first generation of *Geonim* included: Mar bar R' Chanan, Mar R' Mari, Mar R' Huna, R' Chinena and R' Yaakov from Nehar Pakod, R' Ahilai the Levite, R' Huna bar Yosef, R' Chama from Mashan, Mar Yenuka, Ravya bar R' Natronai *(Meiri,* Introduction to *Avos).*

The second generation: Mar R' Yehudai Gaon, who wrote several passages and decisions in the *Gemara* (see above); the book *Halachos Pesukos* is ascribed to him. Also, R' Shmuel bar Mari.

The third generation: R' Shimon Kaira, who wrote *Halachos Gedolos.*

The fourth generation: Mar R' Natronai.

The fifth generation: R' Acha from Shavcha, who wrote *Sefer Hasheiltos.*

The sixth generation: R' Mari the *Kohen,* and R' Tzemach. Anan and Shaul lived at this time. They wrote books against the Talmud and misled many people, until finally their mistakes were discovered and Anan (lit., *cloud)* vanished, and Shaul (similar to שְׁאוֹל, *pit)* 'descended' and did not rise.

The seventh generation: R' Bavi the Levite, R' Chinena bar Mesharshai, R' Malchia, R' Chiya the Levite, R' Yosef bar Shila, and Rav Mordechai the *Kohen.*

The eighth generation: R' Nachshon and R' Moshe the *Kohen.*

The generations continued until the period of R' Saadyah Gaon, who composed many works on the Oral and Written Laws, on grammar, and on some sciences; he also wrote *Sefer Haemunos.* He was a contemporary of David ben Zakkai the *nasi.*

After R' Saadyah came R' Hai bar David, and after him — R' Kohen Zedek and R' Amram.

The generations continued to pass until the era of R' Sherira Gaon, the father of Rabbeinu Hai. R' Sherira was exceedingly wise and pious, and lived to a very old age. He stepped down from his position in the yeshivah, appointing Rabbeinu Hai to succeed him. Thus, R' Sherira lived to see his son rise to greatness, disseminating the Torah throughout the nation and surpassing all the other *Geonim.* He attracted students from all over the world. He was the greatest, and last, of all the *Geonim.* His literary production was vast, including such works as *Sefer Hadinim, Sefer Hashavuos, Sefer Hamekach Umemkar,* and a great number of responsa.

R' Shmuel Hanaggid, who composed *Hilchasa Gevirta* and *Mevo HaTalmud,* was his contemporary, as was R' Shmuel bar Chofni, father-in-law of R' Hai Gaon, who wrote *Shearim Behalachah.*

Also at that time lived the famous Four Captives, through whom the Torah spread across the world. The episode is related in *Seder Hadoros* 4750. The four captives were R' Chushiel, the father of Rabbeinu Chananel; R' Moshe, the father of Rabbeinu Chanoch; R' Shemaryah; and one other whose name is unknown.

Chapter 7
A Review of the Generations

Sages of the Mishnah

(1) Shimon the *Tzaddik* and R' Dosa ben Harkinas *(Rambam*, Introduction to *Mishnah Commentary; Meiri* disagrees).
(2) Antigonus of Socho and R' Elazar ben Charsom.
(3) Yose ben Yoezer and Yose ben Yochanan.
(4) Yehoshua ben Perachyah and Nitai of Arbel; Yochanan ben Mattisyahu the Hasmonean.
(5) Yehudah ben Tabbai and Shimon ben Shatach; Choni Hame'agel (the circle-maker).
(6) Shemayah and Avtalyon; Akavya ben Mahalalel.
(7) Hillel and Shammai; Bava ben Buta.
(8) Rabban Yochanan ben Zakkai, Rabban Gamliel the Elder, and Rabban Shimon, his son.
(9) R' Eliezer and R' Yehoshua, R' Tarfon, Rabban Gamliel, R' Akiva, R' Elazar ben Azaryah, R' Yose of Galilee, R' Yishmael.
(10) R' Meir, R' Yehudah, R' Yose, R' Shimon, R' Nechemiah, R' Elazar ben Yaakov, R' Nehorai, R' Yochanan Hasandlar, R' Shimon ben Gamliel, and R' Eliezer the son of R' Yose of Galilee.
(11) R' Judah the Prince, R' Yishmael bar R' Yose, R' Elazar bar R' Shimon, R' Yose bar Yehudah.

Sages of the Gemara

(1) R' Chiya, Bar Kappara, R' Chanina, R' Efes, R' Oshaya, R' Yannai, Levi, Avuha di *(the father of)* Shmuel, Rav, and Shmuel.

(2) R′ Yochanan, Resh Lakish, R′ Elazar ben Pedas, R′ Yehudah, R′ Huna, R′ Nachman, R′ Adda bar Ahavah, R′ Chananel.
(3) R′ Sheshes, R′ Chisda, Rabbah, R′ Yosef, Ulla, Rabba bar bar Chanah, R′ Chiya bar Abba, R′ Ami, R′ Assi, R′ Abahu, R′ Zeira, R′ Abba.
(4) R′ Yirmiyah, Abaye, Rava, R′ Dimi, Ravin, R′ Safra, R′ Yonah.
(5) R′ Pappa; R′ Huna, the son of R′ Yehoshua; R′ Zevid; R′ Pappi; R′ Kahana; Ameimar; Mar Zutra.
(6) Ravina; R′ Ashi; R′ Acha, the son of Rava; Mereimar.
(7) Mar bar R′ Ashi; Rava Tosfaah, Yehudah bar Mereimar.

Rabbanan Savorai

(1) R′ Sama, the son of Rava; R′ Sama, the son of R′ Yehudai; R′ Achai.
(2) R′ Eina and R′ Simuna.
(3) R′ Ravai Merov.
(4) R′ Giza, R′ Huna, and R′ Dimi Sorgo.

The Geonim

The first generation of *Geonim* began in the year 4349 [589 c.e.], and the first *gaon* was R′ Mari Sorgo, the son of R′ Dimi Sorgo[1] *(Doros Harishonim).* The era of the *Geonim* lasted until the year 4798 [1038 c.e.], concluding with the leadership of R′ Hai Gaon, the son of R′ Sherira Gaon.

See page 80, where we have enumerated the generations of *Geonim* in part.

The Rishonim[2]

(1) The first generation of *Rishonim* (early authorities), who followed the era of *Geonim,* included: Rabbeinu Chananel, who is credited with the authorship of *Sefer Chafetz;* Rabbeinu

1. Cf. page 79, where we presented *Meiri's* view, from his Introduction to *Avos.*

2. [For biographical sketches of each of the sages listed here, see ArtScroll's *The Rishonim.* There are varying opinions regarding the line of demarcation between the Rishonim and Acharonim. Consequently, some of the sages listed here as Acharonim are considered by others as Rishonim.]

Gershom *Meor Hagolah,* (the Light of the Diaspora); and R' Nissim Gaon — all disciples of R' Hai Gaon.

(2) The second generation: R' Yitzchak Alfasi (Rif), a student of Rabbeinu Chananel, Rabbeinu Yaakov ben R' Yakar, a disciple of Rabbeinu Gershom; R' Moshe Hadarshan; R' Nassan of Rome, author of *Aruch;* R' Kelonimus of Rome.

(3) The third generation: Rabbeinu Shlomo Yitzchaki (Rashi), a student of R' Yaakov ben R' Yakar and R' Moshe Hadarshan; R' Yosef (Ri) Migash and Rabbeinu Ephraim, disciples of Rif; R' Avraham Ibn Ezra; R' Yehudah Halevi; and R' Simchah of Vitry, author of *Machzor Vitry,* who was Rashi's student.

(4) The fourth generation: Raavan; Rashbam, Rivam and Rabbeinu Tam, grandsons and disciples of Rashi; and Raavad II (R' Avraham Av Beis Din), author of *HaEshkol.*

(5) The fifth generation: Rambam; R' Zechariah HaLevi, known as the *Baal HaMaor;* Raavad, author of the *Hasagos,* son-in-law of the *Baal HaEshkol;* Ri Hazaken (the Elder), nephew and disciple of Rabbeinu Tam; Rabbeinu Yehonasan; Rabbeinu Eliezer of Metz (מִיץ), a student of Rabbeinu Tam; Rabbeinu Bachya, author of *Chovos Halevavos.*

(6) The sixth generation: Raavyah, a disciple of R' Eliezer of Metz; Rash (R' Shimshon of Sens [שַׁנְץ]), author of *Haterumos,* students of Ri Hazaken; Ramah; Radak; R' Yeshaye of Trani, author of *Tosefos Rid;* R' Yitzchak of Vienna, author of *Ohr Zarua,* a disciple of Raaviah; and the majority of the Tosafists.

(7) The seventh generation: Ramban; Rabbeinu Yonah (Ramban's first cousin); Maharam of Rothenburg, a disciple of *Ohr Zarua.*

(8) The eighth generation: Rashba and Raah, students of Ramban; Rosh; the authors of *Mordechai* and *Hagahos Maimoni,* both of whom studied under Maharam of Rothenburg; Meiri; R' Tzidkiyahu HaRofei, author of *Shibolei Haleket;* and R' Menachem Ricanati.

(9) The ninth generation: Ritva, a student of Raah and Rashba; Ran; R' Yaakov, known as the *Baal HaTurim,* son of the Rosh; R' Vidal of Toulouse, author of *Maggid Mishneh,* and Rabbeinu Yerucham, both disciples of Rosh.

(10) The tenth generation: Rivash, a student of Ran; R' Shimshon ben Tzaddok, author of *Tashbatz;* Abudraham; R' Yosef Chaviva, author of *Nimukei Yosef;* Maharil; R' Yisrael

Isserlein, author of *Terumas Hadeshen.* This was the final generation of *Rishonim.*

The Greatest of the Acharonim

(1) The first generation of *Acharonim* (later authorities): Mahari Weil, a student of Maharil; Rashbash, son of Tashbatz; R' Yitzchak Abarbanel; Mahari Abohav.

(2) The second generation: Maharik; Mahari from Bruna; R' Eliyahu Mizrachi; Maharam Alshakar; Mahari ben Chaviv, author of *Ein Yaakov.*

(3) The third generation: R' Ovadiah from Bertinoro (Rav); Mahari Birav; Maharalbach; Radvaz; Mahari ben Lev.

(4) The fourth generation: Beis Yoseph, a student of Mahari Birav; Mabbit; Rama; Maharshal; Maharshdam; R' Betzalel Ashkenazi, a disciple of Radvaz; Arizal; Rama from Pano; Maharam from Padova; and Maharash Alkabetz.

(5) The fifth generation: Maharitz, the son of the Mabbit; Sma *(Sefer Meiras Einayim)* and *Levush,* disciples of Rama and Maharshal; Maharal of Prague; *Shelah;* Maharsha; Maharam of Lublin; *Bach.*

(6) The sixth generation: Taz, son-in-law of the *Bach; Tosefos Yom Tov,* a student of the Maharal of Prague; *Shach; Birkas Hazevach; Chelkas Mechokek; Magen Avraham.*

(7) The seventh generation: *Beis Shmuel; Shevus Yaakov; Eliyahu Rabba; Chavas Yair; Chacham Tzvi; Kav Hayashar,* the son of *Birkas Hazevach; Panim Meiros,* grandson of *Shach*'s sister; *Ohr Hachaim.*

(8) The eighth generation: *Pnei Yehoshua, Nodah beYehudah;* R' Yonasan Eibshitz, a disciple of *Panim Meiros; Machtzis Hashekel;* R' Moshe Chaim Luzzato; Baal Shem Tov; Maggid of Mezeritch; Yaavetz (R' Yaakov Emden); *Pnei Moshe; Shaagas Aryeh;* the Vilna Gaon, a disciple of the *Pnei Moshe.*

Chapter Eight
Names and Titles of Talmudic Sages

(1) אֲבוּהָ דִשְׁמוּאֵל — *the father of Shmuel:* His name was Abba bar Abba the *Kohen.*

(2) אַבָּיֵי — *Abaye:* His name was Nachmani (see page 69).

(3) אַחֵר — *the other one:* This is Elisha ben Avuyah, the great scholar who turned to apostasy, as recounted in *Chagigah* 15a.

(4) אֲחֵרִים אוֹמְרִים — *others say:* R' Meir is intended. Some, however, contend that only when R' Meir repeats a teaching of his master, Elisha ben Avuyah, who is called אַחֵר, *the other one,* is this expression used.

(5) ר' אֱלִיעֶזֶר — *R' Eliezer:* If the name *R' Eliezer* appears in a mishnah without a father's name, it refers to R' Eliezer ben Hyrkanos, a disciple of R' Yochanan ben Zakkai. He was also called R' Eliezer the Great.

(6-7) ר' אֶלְעָזָר — *R' Elazar:* If a Tanna is meant, he is R' Elazar ben Shamua the Kohen, a contemporary of Rabban Gamliel; if an Amora is meant, he is R' Elazar ben Pedas, a disciple of R' Yochanan.

(8) אֲמוֹרָאֵי דִנְהַרְדְּעָא — *the Amoraim of Nehardea:* R' Chama.

(9) אֲמוֹרָאֵי דִפּוּמְבְּדִיתָא — *the Amoraim of Pumbedisa:* Rabbah and R' Yosef.

(10) אִמְרֵי בֵּי רַב — *they said in the school of Rav:* R' Huna; others hold: R' Hamnuna *(Rashi, Tos.* to *Sanhedrin* 17a).

(11) אִמְרֵי בְּמַעֲרָבָא — *they said in the West:* R' Yirmiyah.

(12) אָמְרוּ עָלָיו בְּמַעֲרָבָא — *they said about it in the West:* R' Chanina *(Halichos Olam).*

(13) אַרְיוֹךְ — *Aryoch:* A nickname for Shmuel.

(14) בֵּית שַׁמַּאי וּבֵית הִלֵּל — *the House of Shammai and the House of Hillel:* This refers to the students of Shammai and of Hillel, since one's students are considered members of his household.

(15) בֶּן בַּג בַּג — *Ben Bag Bag:* R' Yochanan.

(16) בֶּן בְּתֵירָא — *Ben Beseira:* Three who held the office of *nasi* during the Temple era bore this surname — R' Yehoshua, R' Shimon, and R' Yehudah *(Eduyyos* 8:1).

(17-19) בֶּן עַזַּאי, בֶּן זוֹמָא, בֶּן נַנָּס — *Ben Azzai, Ben Zoma, Ben Nannas:* the first name of each was Shimon.

(20) בְּנָן שֶׁל קְדוֹשִׁים — *son of holy men.* R' Menachem bar Simai was accorded this title, because he was careful not to glance even at a figure on a coin.

(21) בַּר פַּחֲתֵי — *Bar Pachasei:* R' Chiya called his nephew, Rav, by this appellative, which means, *son of great ancestors.*

(22) רַבָּן גַּמְלִיאֵל הַזָּקֵן — *Rabban Gamliel the Elder:* He was the son of R' Shimon ben Hillel the Elder.

(23) רַבָּן גַּמְלִיאֵל דְיַבְנֶה — *Rabban Gamliel of Yavneh:* He was the son of R' Shimon ben Gamliel, one of the עֲשָׂרָה הֲרוּגֵי מַלְכוּת, *ten martyrs executed by the Romans.* R' Gamliel's brother-in-law was R' Eliezer ben Hyrkanos. Any mention of *R' Gamliel* without a patronymic refers to him.

(24) דַּיָּינֵי אֶרֶץ יִשְׂרָאֵל — *the judges of Eretz Yisrael:* R' Ami and R' Assi.

(25) דַּיָּינֵי גוֹלָה — *the judges of the Exile:* Karna.

(26) דַּיָּינֵי דִנְהַרְדְעָא — *the judges of Nehardea:* R' Adda bar Minyomi.

(27) דַּיָּינֵי דְסוּרָא — *the judges of Sura:* R' Huna and R' Yitzchak *(Halichos Olam).*

(28) דַּיָּינֵי דְפוּמְבְּדִיתָא — *the judges of Pumbedisa:* R' Pappa bar Shmuel.

(29) הַדָּנִין לִפְנֵי חֲכָמִים — *Those who discuss before the Sages:* This refers to Shimon ben Azzai, Shimon ben Zoma, Chanan the Egyptian, and Chananyah ben Chachinai. *Rambam* substitutes Chananyah of Ono for the fourth sage. R' Nachman bar Yitzchak adds Shimon HaTimni[1] to the list, and *Rambam* writes Shimon ben Nanas instead.

(30) הִלֵּל הַנָּשִׂיא — *Hillel the Prince:* Son of R' Judah the Prince. He

1. [The appellation *HaTimni* was given him because he was from the city of Timnas *(Rashi* to *Beitzah* 21a).]

introduced the practice of intercalation into the calendar, and was a contemporary of Abaye and Rava, ten generations after Hillel the Elder. Others contend that he lived fourteen generations afterwards; this is the more accurate opinion (see *Doros Harishonim).*

(31) ר׳ זֵירָא — *R' Zeira:* Before he immigrated to Eretz Yisrael, he had the title *Rav.* After arriving in Eretz Yisrael he was ordained, and thereafter was awarded the title *Rabbi.*

(32) חֲבִיבַי — *Chavivai:* Rav called his uncle, R' Chiya — who was a brother to both his father and mother *(Pesachim* 4a; see *Rashi* ad loc.) — by this contraction of the Hebrew expression אַח אָבִי, *brother of my father.*

(33) חֲכָמִים אוֹמְרִים — *the Sages say:* This pluralized form may introduce the teaching of a single sage, since, as *Rambam* (Introduction to *Mishnah Commentary,* ch. 6) explains, many received the teaching from this sage.

(34) חָסִיד אֶחָד — *a pious one:* R' Yehudah the son of R' Ilai, or R' Yehudah ben Bava.

(35) חֲסִידֵי בָבֶל — *the pious ones of Babylon:* R' Huna and R' Chisda *(Taanis* 23b).

(36) חֲרִיפֵי דְפוּמְבְּדִיתָא — *the keen intellects of Pumbedisa:* Eifa and Avimi, the sons of Rechava.

(37) טַבְיוֹמִי — *Tavyomi:* Nickname for Mar bar R' Ashi *(Bava Basra* 12b). However, he is not the R' Tavyomi found throughout the Talmud.

(38) רַב יְהוּדָה — *Rav Yehudah:* Without a father's name, he is R' Yehudah bar Yechezkel.

(39) ר׳ יְהוּדָה — *R' Yehudah:* Without a patronymic, reference is made to R' Yehudah the son of R' Ilai, who was always given the honor of being the first speaker.

(40) ר׳ יְהוּדָה נְשִׂיאָה — *R' Yehudah Nesiah:* He was a *nasi,* the son of Rabban Gamliel and grandson of R' Judah the Prince. He was an *Amora.* All told, three men bore the name and title, R' Judah the Prince. (This is clearly proven in *Doros Harishonim.)*

(41) ר׳ יְהוֹשֻׁעַ — *R' Yehoshua:* If this name appears in a mishnah without a patronymic, it refers to R' Yehoshua ben Chananya, the disciple of R' Yochanan ben Zakkai. He was a Levite who sang in the Temple.

(42) ר׳ יְהוֹשֻׁעַ בֶּן קָרְחָה — *R' Yehoshua ben Karchah:* Karchah is R'

Akiva, and R′ Yehoshua was his son. Others dispute this, however.

(43) ר׳ יוֹסֵי — *R′ Yose:* Without a patronymic, he is R′ Yose ben Chalafta.

(44) יֵשׁ אוֹמְרִים — *some say:* In the majority of cases this refers to R′ Nassan *(Tos.* to *Bava Basra* 15b, s.v. וי״א).

(45) לְמֵידִין לִפְנֵי חֲכָמִים — *it was argued before the Sages:* Levi before Rabbi, or Levi and the students of his yeshivah before Rabbi. The foregoing applies only when the phrase is found in a מֵימְרָא, *private teaching,* but if found in a *baraisa,* Levi is not meant *(Rashi* to *Me'ilah* 9b disputes this; see *Tos.* ad loc.). Mention of Levi without a patronymic refers to Levi ben Sisi.

(46) ר׳ מֵאִיר — *R′ Meir:* His name was R′ Miasha or R′ Misha, but he was called R′ Meir because he enlightened (מֵאִיר) the Sages in the Halachah. Besides R′ Meir, one other *Tanna* and one *Amora* were also named R′ Miasha.

(47) מַחֲכוּ עֲלָהּ בְּמַעֲרָבָא — *They laughed at it in the West:* R′ Yose, the son of R′ Chanina.

(48) מָרָא דְאַרְעָא דְיִשְׂרָאֵל — *The Master of Eretz Yisrael:* R′ Elazar ben Pedas.

(49) מִשּׁוּם ר׳ יִשְׁמָעֵאל אָמַר תַּלְמִיד אֶחָד לִפְנֵי ר׳ עֲקִיבָא — *one student spoke in the name of R′ Yishmael before R′ Akiva:* This refers to R′ Meir, who studied under both scholars.

(50) ר׳ נְהוֹרָאי — *R′ Nehorai:* R′ Elazar ben Arach was also known as R′ Nehorai and R′ Nechemiah. However, I have heard that *R′ Nehorai* and *R′ Nechemiah* usually refer to two of R′ Akiva's disciples. Some *Amoraim* were also named R′ Nehorai and R′ Nechemiah.

(51) נְהַרְבְּלָאֵי מַתְנֵי — *the Neharbeleans teach:* Rami bar Berabi; according to another version: bar Barochi *(Rashi* to *Beitzah* 8b).

(52) ר׳ נַחְמָן — *R′ Nachman:* When mentioned without a patronymic, this refers to R′ Nachman bar Yaakov *(Tos.* to *Bava Basra* 46b), who married into the family of the *nasi.*

(53) סָבֵי דְבֵי רַב — *the Elders of the School of Rav:* R′ Huna; according to others: R′ Hamnuna.

(54) סָבֵי דְסוּרָא — *the Elders of Sura:* R′ Huna and R′ Chisda.

(55) סָבֵי דְפוּמְבְּדִיתָא — *the Elders of Pumbedisa:* R′ Yehudah and R′ Eina.

(56) סִינַי — *Sinai:* R' Yosef *(Berachos* 64a), who knew the mishnayos as clearly as when they were given at Sinai (cf. *Rashi* ibid.).

(57) עוֹקֵר הָרִים — *one who uproots mountains:* Rabbah, the colleague of R' Yosef, was so named because of his extraordinarily keen and penetrating intellect *(Berachos* ibid., *Rashi* ad loc.).

(58) קְהָלָא קַדִּישָׁה — *the holy assembly.* This group included R' Shimon ben Menasya and R' Yose ben Meshulam, who earned their title of distinction because they used to divide their days into three parts — one-third for prayer, one-third for Torah study, and one-third for work *(Koheles Rabbah* to 9:9). *Aruch* writes that they toiled in Torah during the winter months and earned their living during the summer.

(59) קְטִינָא חֲרִיךְ שַׁקֵי — *the small one with the burnt leg:* R' Zeira, who was small and whose leg had been singed by fire.

(60) רַב — *Rav:* R' Abba, the colleague of Shmuel.

(61) רָבָא — *Rava* (without a patronymic): The son of R' Yosef bar Chama.

(62) רַבָּה — *Rabbah* (without a patronymic): Rabbah bar Nachmani.[2]

(63) רַבּוֹתֵינוּ שֶׁבְּאֶרֶץ יִשְׂרָאֵל — *our Rabbis in Eretz Yisrael:* R' Abba.

(64) רַבּוֹתֵינוּ שֶׁבְּבָבֶל — *our Rabbis in Babylon:* Rav and Shmuel.

(65) רַבִּי — *Rabbi* (teacher par excellence), *Rabbeinu HaKadosh* (our holy teacher): R' Judah the Prince.

(66) שָׁבוּר מַלְכָּא — *Shavor Malka (King Shavor):* A surname of Shmuel *(Pesachim* 54a; see *Rashi* ad loc.).

(67) שִׁינְנָא — *keen scholar:* Shmuel called his disciple, R' Yehudah, by this descriptive appellation.

(68) שָׁלְחוּ מִתָּם — *they sent from there:* R' Elazar.

(69) ר' שִׁמְעוֹן — *R' Shimon* (without a patronymic): R' Shimon ben Yochai, the disciple of R' Akiva.

(70) שָׁקוּד — *diligent one:* A surname of Shmuel.

---

2. *Aruch* (s.v. 'Abaye') cites *R' Sherira Gaon* and *R' Hai Gaon* that both Rabbah and Rava were each named R' Abba; however, in both cases the name was contracted — one to Rabbah and the other to Rava. Later commentators explain that the reason the two names were contracted differently is because Rabbah's real name was אַבָּה, with the letter ה at the end of the word, while Rava's name was spelled אַבָא, with an א at the end. Thus, in order that the names of these two great sages should not be confused, they called one Rabbah, with a *dagesh* (dot) in the letter *beis*, and the other Rava, without a *dagesh*.

(71) תָּנָא דְבֵי אֵלִיָּהוּ — *the Academy of Eliyahu taught:* Reference is not to the prophet Elijah, but to a *Tanna* bearing that name who is mentioned in *Rambam's Mishnah Commentary (Yad Malachi; Seder Hadoros).* Others disagree *(Tos.* to *Shabbos* 13b, s.v. בימי).

(72) תָּנֵי ר׳ סַפְרָא מִשּׁוּם חַד דְּבֵי רַב — *R' Safra taught, citing one from the House of Rabbi:* This refers to R' Gamliel, the most outstanding of his sons.

❦ ❦ ❦

Many sages who are mentioned in either Talmud in regard to only one halachah or to only one homiletical passage are called after that halachah or homily. For example, to the mishnah that teaches that the finding of coins left in a pile must be announced, R' Yitzchak adds the qualification: *This is true, provided they are like pyramids* — i.e., the larger coins are on the bottom and progressively smaller ones are on top of them, indicating an intentional placement which the owner can later identify *(Bava Metzia* 25a). Consequently, he is called R' Yitzchak Migdelaah *(migdal* means *pyramid* or *tower).*

The sage, R' Zuhamai, was so named because he taught the rule that just as a person who is dirty *(mezuham)* is unfit for the Temple service, so dirty hands disqualify one from reciting Grace *(Berachos* 53b). Likewise, another sage was called Ben Rechumi *(Nazir* 13a) because of the two questions he posed to Abaye. One involved a person who says, 'I undertake to become a Nazirite when I have a son'; hence, *ben* (son). The second involved a similar question about a friend (hence, *rechumi).*

There are many more examples of this *(Maharatz Chayos* in his glosses to the Talmud).

Chapter Nine
Principles for Deciding the Law

These principles apply only (a) when the Talmud itself does not establish the halachah in any given passage, and (b) in the majority of cases.

General Rules

(1) The common opinion of several sages prevails against the opinion of an individual.

(2) The halachah follows an anonymous mishnah, even against an anonymous *baraisa,* and certainly when the *baraisa* contains a dispute between authorities.

(3) If an anonymous mishnah [containing only one opinion] precedes one containing a dispute, the halachah does not follow the anonymous mishnah. But if the anonymous mishnah is recorded after the mishnah with the dispute, the halachah is in accordance with the anonymous mishnah. The above is true only when the two mishnayos appear separately in the text; but if they appear in tandem, the order is insignificant[1] *(Sefer Hakerisus).*

(4) The above rule (3) applies only if both mishnayos are located in the same tractate, but if they are found in different tractates their order is insignificant. However, if the anonymous mishnah and the one containing the dispute appear in different orders (e.g., one is in *Zeraim* and the other in *Moed),* some authorities

1. With this principle I have resolved the difficulty posed by *Maharam Shif* on *Maharam's* commentary to *Tos., Bava Metzia* 2a, s.v. שנים.

contend that the order is significant, since the six individual orders were arranged in a specific sequence. Others regard *Bava Kamma, Bava Metzia* and *Bava Basra* as one long tractate called *Nezikin,* which was divided into three parts, and thus the order of the mishnayos contained therein is significant. Further, some *Rishonim* (see *Yad Malachi* §338) consider the entire Order of *Nezikin* as one long tractate with regard to rule (3).

(5) Every mishnah in Tractate Eduyyos — also called *Bechirta* (see p. 101) — is actual law.

(6) The halachah follows the more lenient view in the laws of mourning, even when it is the opinion of a single authority against the common view of many, except regarding קְרִיעָה, *rending the garment.*

(7) The halachah follows the more lenient view in the laws of *eruvin* even if it represents the opinion of one authority against that of many *(Eruvin* 46a).

(8) The halachah follows a third authority who sides with one of two disputants (see p. 108).

(9) The law does not follow a *shitah* (a group of sages who share a common opinion; see ch. 10 §48). Others dispute this.

(10) In a dispute between the Babylonian *(Bavli)* and Jerusalem *(Yerushalmi)* Talmuds, the halachah follows the former. The *Rishonim* explain that *Bavli* was composed after *Yerushalmi,* and the accepted rule requires that the law be decided according to the later opinion (see *Maharatz Chayos* to *Taanis* 16a).

(11) If the *Gemara* states a halachah anonymously (as undisputed), this is the actual law, even if elsewhere it is disputed by *Amoraim,* and even if one of the disputing *Amoraim* is one whom the halachah always follows according to the rules of the *Gemara.*

(12) We do not decide the law directly from *Tosefta, Baraisa, Sifra* or *Sifrei,* but only according to the teachings of the *Amoraim* in the *Gemara.*

(13) We do not derive the law from *Midrash* or *Aggadah,* nor does *Aggadah* supersede the legal discourses of the *Gemara.* However, when the *midrashim* and *aggados* do not contradict the Talmud, but rather augment it, then we may learn from and rely on them.

Rules Regarding Disputes between Tannaim

(1) The halachah generally follows Beis Hillel over Beis Shammai, except in (a) specific cases when the Sages point out that the law is like neither, and (b) the six cases when the law follows the view of Beis Shammai (some say that there are only three such instances).

(2) The opinion of Beis Shammai, when opposed by Beis Hillel, has no status as a mishnah. It is not considered like an anonymous mishnah which precedes a mishnah with a dispute (in which case the halachah does not follow the anonymous statement); in fact, it is less significant than even a single authority against a plurality.

(3) The halachah never agrees with the opinion of R' Eliezer ben Hyrkanos, because he was שַׁמּוּתִי.[2]

(4) The halachah follows R' Akiva against any single adversary, but not against two or more.

(5) The teaching of R' Elazar ben Yaakov is קַב וְנָקִי, *small but good,* and the ruling always follows his opinion. Rabbeinu Chananel cites a tradition that in 102 (the numerical value of קַב) disputed matters the halachah follows R' Elazar ben Yaakov.

(6) In a dispute between R' Yehudah and R' Nechemiah, the halachah follows the latter. *Rambam* does not accept this rule (see *Hil. Avodas Yom Hakippurim* 5:1, *Kesef Mishnah* ad loc.).

(7) In a dispute between R' Yehudah and R' Shimon, the halachah follows the former.

(8) R' Yehudah's opinions regarding *eruvin* are law, but not regarding מְחִיצוֹת, *partitions,* that enclose an area and make it permissible to carry there on the Sabbath.

---

2. The *Rishonim* advance three interpretations of this term: *Rashi* writes that R' Eliezer was excommunicated by his colleagues *(Bava Metzia* 59b). *Aruch* and *Tosafos* contend that he was not actually banned, but that he was considered as one of the disciples of Beis Shammai (שַׁמּוּתִי = שַׁמַּאי). That is, even though he was actually a student of R' Yochanan ben Zakkai, who himself was a disciple of Beis Hillel, nevertheless the Talmud considers all of R' Eliezer's opinions as coinciding with those of Beis Shammai (i.e., the halachah does not follow his views). *Ritva* interprets the expression to mean that R' Eliezer adopted Beis Shammai's habit of taking issue with the majority opinion.

(9) The halachah does not follow R' Meir, because his reasoning was too deep for his colleagues to fathom. His decrees which provided for a stricter application of Biblical law were accepted, but not his penalties and fines.

(10) The halachah is in accordance with R' Yose against all his colleagues, since he had sound reasons for his rulings. *Rashi* (*Eruvin* 51a) explains that his logic was straightforward. *Rambam's* version is that R' Yose's opinion is preferred over one colleague, but not over two or more.

(11) The halachah follows any opinion of R' Shimon ben Gamliel which appears in a mishnah (not in a *baraisa),* with the exception of three cases.[3] This rule is not universally accepted.

(12) The halachah follows Rabbi against any single opponent, with the exception of his father. Some contend that Rabbi's view prevails even against that of his father.

Rules Regarding Disputes between Amoraim

(1) In a legal dispute between Rav and Shmuel regarding civil law, the halachah follows Shmuel's opinion. In ritual law, it follows Rav — with three exceptions regarding which Shmuel's view prevails *(Shabbos* 22a).

(2) R' Yochanan's view prevails over that of Rav.

(3) R' Yochanan's view prevails over that of Shmuel.

(4) When Rav and Shmuel together oppose R' Yochanan, some adopt R' Yochanan's view, while others follow Rav and Shmuel, since they form a majority.

---

3. [They are:

(a) Even if a lender stipulates the right to collect directly from the guarantor, he may not do so, according to R' Shimon, if the borrower himself has the wherewithal to pay. The Rabbis hold that he may go directly to the guarantor for payment, as per the condition *(Bava Basra* 10:7).

(b) If one gives his wife a *get* (bill of divorce) on condition that she return his coat to him, and she subsequently loses the coat, R' Shimon maintains that she may effectively fulfill the condition by remitting the cash value of the coat. The Rabbis argue that she can fulfill the condition only by returning the item *(Gittin* 7:5).

(c) R' Shimon holds that a judgment in court may be overturned to allow a defeated litigant to bring new witnesses or proofs. The Rabbis contend that the judgment concludes the proceedings *(Sanhedrin* 3:5).]

(5) R' Yochanan's view prevails over that of Resh Lakish, with three exceptions.[4]
(6) The halachah always follows R' Yehoshua ben Levi.
(7) In a dispute between R' Huna and R' Nachman, the former's view prevails in matters of ritual law and the latter's in civil law.
(8) In a dispute between R' Sheshes and R' Nachman, the former's view prevails in matters of ritual law and the latter's in civil law.
(9) R' Yehudah's opinion prevails over Rabbah's.
(10) In a disagreement between Rabbah and R' Yosef based upon their own analyses of the issues, and not upon traditions they received from their teachers, the halachah follows Rabbah[5] — with three exceptions.[6] Some contend that this principle applies only to disputes between Rabbah and R' Yosef which appear in *Bava Basra.*
(11) Rava's opinion prevails over that of Abaye, except in six cases (see p. 70).

---

4. [They are:

(a) In the case of a *yavam* (a man whose childless brother died, requiring him to marry the brother's widow or release her through a mechanism called *chalitzah;* see *Deut.* 25:5*ff)* who had performed *chalitzah* with his brother's pregnant widow, and she subsequently miscarried, R' Yochanan holds that the *chalitzah* need not be repeated, while Resh Lakish maintains that it must be *(Yevamos* 35b).

(b) When a testator awards one field to someone as a gift, and another field to a second person as an inheritance, R' Yochanan holds that both acquire possession, while Resh Lakish disagrees *(Bava Basra* 129a).

(c) If one assigns his estate in writing to his son, and the son later sells the estate and then dies while the father is still alive, R' Yochanan says that the buyer does not acquire ownership, while Resh Lakish holds that he does (ibid. 136a).]

5. Because Rabbah 'uprooted mountains' — that is, his analysis and reasoning were sharper than R' Yosef's, who was famed for his broad range of knowledge (see *Berachos* 64a, *Rashi* ad loc.; see ch. 8 §56, 57).

6. [They are:

(a) When heirs divide an estate, and one of them owns land adjacent to one border of the estate, Rabbah maintains that the other heirs must give him his share next to his own property, while R' Yosef argues that the other heirs can put a higher valuation on that land and demand compensation accordingly *(Bava Basra* 12b).

(b) With regard to symbolical acquisition, which binds a party or parties to an agreement, Rabbah holds that any of the parties may withdraw as long as the court that dealt with the matter is in session. R' Yosef maintains that withdrawal is possible only as long as they are actually dealing with that subject (ibid. 114a).

(c) If a testator expressed his wish that his estate be divided between his wife and his son, R' Yosef holds that the widow is entitled to half the estate, even though she is not a legal heir; Rabbah disagrees (ibid. 143a).]

(12) R' Ashi's opinion is accepted over that of Ravina.

(13) Throughout the Talmud, when Ravina and R' Acha argue, the former consistently adopts the more lenient view, while the latter takes the stricter position, and the halachah follows Ravina. In three cases, however, Ravina adopts the stricter view, and the law is in accordance with R' Acha.[7]

(14) The law always follows Mar bar R' Ashi, except in the two instances (see page 73). Others maintain that, on the contrary, only in those two cases does the halachah follow his view.

(15) The halachah is always in accordance with the later opinion, except when a student disagrees with his master. This rule applies only up to the generation before Abaye and Rava. However, from the time of Abaye and Rava the later opinion always prevails, even in the case of a student who disputes his master.

Inferring the Halachah from the Terminology

(1) The expression זֶה הַכְּלָל, *this is the principle,* indicates that the halachah is so.

(2) The expression קָסָבַר, *he thought,* introduces the opinion of a *Tanna* or *Amora* which the halachah does not follow.

(3) The term תֵּיקוּ, *teiku,* indicates that the Talmud is in doubt as to the halachah. With regard to a case involving monetary claims, the procedure is to dismiss the claim. With regard to a ritual law of Biblical origin, we adopt the stricter approach. If the case involves a Rabbinic ritual law, we tend to be lenient.

(4) When the *Gemara* explicitly posits an assumption during a halachic discourse with the expression אִם תִּמְצֵי לוֹמַר, *if you can say,* that assumption is law *(Rambam,* following a tradition from the *Geonim).* But if this term is not actually stated, although the idea is implied, the rule does not apply *(Ran* to *Kiddushin* 7b).

---

7. [Regarding the case of dark red meat, if it is cut up and salted and placed on the coals, R' Acha and Ravina disagree: R' Acha holds that the coals will draw out the blood (and the meat would be permitted), and Ravina maintains that they will cause the meat to contract, so that the blood will not flow out and the meat is therefore forbidden. Similar disputes exists regarding the testicles and regarding the arteries *(Chullin* 93b).]

(5) When the *Gemara* cites two divergent statements, using such terminology as אִיכָּא דְאַמְרֵי, *there are those who say;* אִיכָּא דְמַתְנֵי, *there are those who learn it;* or אִי בָּעֵית אֵימָא, *if you wish, I shall say,* some *Rishonim* maintain that R' Ashi intentionally placed the correct statement of the law last, in order to conclude the discourse with the principal opinion. According to these *Rishonim,* this is an absolute rule, to be applied both in Biblical as well as Rabbinical law, and even if it results in a stringent ruling *(Ritz* [*R' Yitzchak Ibn*] *Gias;* see *Ran* to *Avodah Zarah* 7a). However, others opine that R' Ashi's method was to first state the principal, majority opinion, which is the halachah, and then cite the minority opinion. In fact, the statement of any minority or secondary opinion is prefaced with the words יֵשׁ אוֹמְרִים, *there are those who say.* There are also other views *(Riva;* see *Rosh* to *Avodah Zarah* ibid.) regarding this rule.

Chapter Ten
Terminology of the Talmud

(1) אַגָּדָה, הַגָּדָה — Any passage in the Talmud not dealing with the halachos involving the performance of *mitzvos,* but with matters of ethics and morality or the reasons for the commandments, is called *Aggadah,* and when such a passage conflicts with another containing halachic interpretation the *Aggadah* must not be followed. It is important to understand that many *aggados* defy literal interpretation. We are obligated to believe that the righteous and holy Sages who bequeathed the rich Oral Tradition of *Aggadah* to us intentionally did so in the form of allusions and hidden mysteries, which in fact bespeak matters of the highest supernal nature. However, since our Sages did not wish to reveal these secrets to the common people, they clothed them in the outer garments of simple tales; the deeper meanings lie beneath for the intellectually inquisitive to uncover.[1]

R' Simlai stated: I have a tradition from my forefathers that one should not teach *Aggadah* to a Babylonian or to someone from the South, since they are haughty and unlearned and therefore interpret the teaching according to their personal desires, and they do not perceive the truth *(Yerushalmi* to *Pesachim* 5:3).

---

1. These matters are explained by *Rambam's Mishnah Commentary* in the Introduction and to *Sanhedrin* 11:1, *Rashba, Hakosev* to *Ein Yaakov (Berachos 6a),* and *Shelah (Torah Shebe'al peh).*

(2) אִיבַּעְיָא לְהוּ, *they asked:* This term indicates that one group of sages is questioning another group of sages.

בָּעוּ מִינֵּיהּ, *they asked of him:* Several sages are asking one.

בְּעָא מִינֵּיהּ, *he asked of him:* One sage asks another.

(3) אֵין לְמֵדִין מִן הַכְּלָלוֹת, *one cannot ascertain the halachah from general rules:* This applies only to general rules taught by *Tannaim,* for they were expressed with great brevity, but those taught by *Amoraim* may be followed, since the *Amoraim* explained these general rules well (see *Eruvin* 66a, *Tos.* ad loc., s.v. כל מקום, and *Rashash* ibid.).

(4) אִיתְּמַר, *it is stated:* This term is used only in regard to a controversy between *Amoraim.* However, in *Yoma* (57b) it is mentioned in a dispute between the *Tannaim,* R' Yoshayah and R' Yonasan. *Ritva* there explains that their dispute was never actually taught in a mishnah or *baraisa,* but that the *Amoraim* had received it as a tradition, which they subsequently repeated in the Academy. *Tosafos Yeshanim* there suggest that the use of אִיתְּמַר was justified because R' Yoshayah and R' Yonasan were among the final *Tannaim.*

(5) אַל תִּקְרֵי, *do not read:* This expression for the most part tells us not to read this word as it appears, but as such ... i.e., interchanging one letter for another, or one vowel sound for another. For example: Do not read שַׁמּוֹת, *desolations,* but שֵׁמוֹת, *names (Berachos* 7b); read not: *There is none* (בִּלְתֶּךָ) *besides You,* but *there is none* (בַּלֹּתֶךָ) *to consume You* (ibid. 10b).

The *Gemara* (ibid. 30b) teaches us that one should stand to pray only in a reverent frame of mind, for it is written, *Prostrate yourselves before HASHEM in the beauty of holiness (Psalms* 29:2). Read not הַדְרַת, *beauty,* but חֶרְדַּת, *trembling. Maharatz Chayos* cites *Yerushalmi* (to *Shabbos,* ch. 7), explaining that the Sages were not reluctant to interchange the letters ה and ח, since in their day the ה was written like the ח, with the left leg touching the roof of the letter.

However, *Rambam (Moreh Nevuchim* 3:43) writes that every אַל תִּקְרֵי interpretation in the Talmud is only of a metaphorical nature, whereby the Scriptural verses are used as a mnemonic device (see *Eruvin* 21b), but not that the Torah actually intended the change. This view parallels *Rambam's* opinion of the

אַסְמַכְתָּא, discussed above (cf. *Maharatz Chayos* to *Rosh Hashanah* 13b, who disagrees).

(6) אֶלָּא, *rather:* This term signals the Talmud's regret for and intention to abandon a prior opinion. Thus, it is used only when an *Amora* is specifically identified with the earlier opinion. However, if no such identification is made, the prior opinion is not regarded as an actual position that must now be abandoned, but only as part of an ongoing dialectic. Hence, the use of אֶלָּא would be inappropriate. *R' Betzalel Ashkenazi* writes in *Shitah Mekubetzes* that occasionally אֶלָּא is used even without prior mention of an *Amora,* but that with prior mention אֶלָּא is always employed.

(7) אִלְמָלֵא, *if it were not;* אִלְמָלֵי, *if it were.*

(8) אָמַר מַר, *the distinguished one said:* This expression introduces the words of a *Tanna,* while גּוּפָא, *the text says,* is used in reference to an *Amora's* teaching.

Rashi (Sukkah 14a, s.v. משו״ה) writes: I asked my teacher if it was possible to apply the term גּוּפָא to a mishnah that was mentioned in passing, as we do to the statements of *Amoraim,* and my master told me that the mishnah in question was from the Order of *Taharos,* which has no *Gemara* to explain it as the other orders of the Mishnah do, and so the Talmud is wont to say גּוּפָא regarding such mishnayos in order to elucidate them.

Nevertheless, we find instances of the rule's inversion: the use of אָמַר מַר as a preface to the statements of *Amoraim,* and גּוּפָא to introduce a *Tanna's* statement.

(9) אָמַר פְּלוֹנִי, *said So-and-so:* The cited authority does not dispute what has been stated.

פְּלוֹנִי אָמַר, *So-and-so said:* Usually this twist of phraseology indicates that the cited authority disputes a previous statement.

(10) אָמַר ר׳ פְּלוֹנִי, אָמַר ר׳ פְּלוֹנִי, *Rabbi ... said, quoting Rabbi ...:* The former did not actually hear the teaching from the latter, but from another who did. (There are many contradictions to this rule. See Introduction to *Seder Hadoros.)*

(11) אַתְקְפְתָּא: This term, which is expressed as מַתְקִיף לָהּ, indicates a question. However, the *Amora* does not challenge his colleague's statement on the basis of a mishnah or *baraisa,* but on the strength of his own reasoning and analysis. Nevertheless, we also find this expression used when an

Amora challenges a mishnah or *baraisa* (see *Chagigah* 5b; *Bava Metzia* 33b; *Rashi* ad loc.).

(12) בֶּאֱמֶת אָמְרוּ, *in truth they said.* A halachah introduced by this expression has the status of הֲלָכָה לְמשֶׁה מִסִּינַי, *an oral tradition originating at Sinai (Rav* to *Terumos* 2:1); see below §25.

(13) בּוּרְכָא, *an absurdity (Rashi* to *Shevuos* 12b); *worthless* (op. cit. *Kesubos* 63b); *unfounded* (op. cit. *Chullin* 88b). This exclamation may be directed only at an *Amora* who ventures a novel opinion based upon his own interpretation *(Yad Malachi).*

(14) בְּחִירְתָּא — A surname of Tractate *Eduyyos.* Some contend that the name *Eduyyos* does not derive from עֵדוּת, *testimony,* but from עִידִית, *choice land;* hence, the tractate's surname is appropriately *Bechirta,* which also means *choice* or *select.*

(15) בְּמַאי קָמִיפַּלְגֵי, *about what are they arguing?* That is, what is the theoretical basis of their legal dispute?

(16) גּוּפָא, *the text itself states:* When the teaching of an *Amora* or a *baraisa* has been mentioned in passing during a Talmudic exposition of another topic, and subsequently the *Gemara* wants to elaborate on that statement or *baraisa* or to question it, it will return to that subject with the expression גּוּפָא, which implies that although originally the teaching only concerned us incidentally, it is now our main interest. On the other hand, the expression אָמַר מַר may be used in returning to a statement that also previously was of chief concern *(Shelah).*

(17) גְּמִירִי לְהוּ, *they taught them:* In the majority of instances, this term refers to a הֲלָכָה לְמשֶׁה מִסִּינַי (see §25).

(18) דִּבְרֵי סוֹפְרִים, *words of the Sages:* Included in this category are traditions received by Moses (see *Rambam, Commentary* to *Kelim* 17:12), Biblical interpretations of the Rabbis *(Sanhedrin* 88b), and Rabbinic decrees and regulations (see *Kiddushin* 39a, *Yevamos* 20b).

(19) דִּבְרֵי קַבָּלָה, *words of tradition:* The Books of the Prophets and the Hagiographa are called thus by the Sages. The *Rishonim* offer two explanations of this expression: The words of the prophets are called words of קַבָּלָה because the prophets used to cry out (קוֹבֵל) to the sinful people about the impending tragedies that were revealed to them in prophetic visions. Others explain that the term signifies that all the prophets

received (קִבְּלוּ) their prophecies from Moses (quoted in *Shitah Mekubetzes* to *Bava Kamma* 2b; see *Maharatz Chayos* to *Taanis* 15a). Nevertheless, we sometimes find that passages from the Prophets are called *Torah* (see *Moed Katan* 5a, *Bava Basra* 147a, et al.), but the *Rishonim* explain that such applications of the term are not intended literally.

(20) דִּבְרֵי תּוֹרָה, *words of the Torah:* Included in this category are laws explicitly stated in the Torah, traditions received by Moses at Sinai (see *Sukkah* 6b, *Rashi* ad loc.; *Berachos* 19b, *Rashi* ad loc.), and Scriptural interpretations (see *Bava Metzia* 48a).

(21) דֵּיקָא נַמִּי, *there is also an evidence:* This expression is used when the proof offered lies within the language or subject matter of the topic under discussion *(Darkei HaGemara* by *R' Yitzchak ben Yaakov Kanpanton).*

(22) הָכִי נַמִּי מִסְתַּבְּרָא, *so, indeed, it stands to reason:* This expression is used to adduce an outside source — such as a mishnah or *baraisa — to support an argument.*

(23) הָכִי קָאָמַר, *this is what he means:* This term indicates that although a statement is defective, nevertheless one may, with difficulty, construe the missing phrase(s) from the text that is extant (see §30; *Darkei HaGemara).*

(24) הֲלָכָה, וְאֵין מוֹרִין כֵּן, *this is the law, but it should not be applied:* Even though the law permits this, we do not follow it in practice, lest it lead to the commission of actual transgressions.

(25) הֲלָכָה לְמֹשֶׁה מִסִּינַי, *a tradition received by Moses at Sinai:* This indicates a rule that is otherwise impossible to derive from Scripture, such as the tort called צְרוֹרוֹת, *stones,* for which half the damages are awarded *(Bava Kamma* 3b). There are many such laws and commandments whose myriad details were given at Sinai, and yet not one hint of them is made in the Written Law.[2]

(26) וּדְקָאָרֵי לָהּ, מַאי קָאָרֵי לָהּ, *and he who asked it, how could he have asked it at all?:* This is a challenge to the questioner, seeking to discover what he was thinking, inasmuch as the answer to his query appears to be obvious. Some believe that this expression originated with the *Rabbanan Savorai* (because the language is

---

2. See *Addendum* at the end of this chapter.

different than the *Gemara's* usual phraseology). *Maharik* cites *Aruch* as stating that the *aleph* in קָאָרֵי is interchanged with an *ayin*, resulting in a word which means *mixture* (קָעָרֵי, from עִרוּי). Thus, the gist of the full expression is: What prompted you to confound this with that?

(27) וְהָא אִיתְּמַר, *but it has been said;* וְהָא תְּנַן, *but we learned;* תְּנַן, *we learned;* וּרְמִינְהוּ, *a contradiction is shown;* וְהָתַנְיָא, *but it is taught;* אֵינִי, *is it so?;* הֲוִי בָּה, *think about it;* וְהָוִינַן בָּה, *and we thought about it.* These are all used for a refutation. Nevertheless, וְהָתַנְיָא often introduces a *baraisa* brought in support of the previous statement, and in the majority of cases וְהָא תַּנְיָא is also employed when adducing proof.

(28) וּרְמִינְהוּ, *a contradiction is shown:* This expression is similar to רָמָה בַיָּם, *He hurled into the sea (Ex.* 15:1). Thus, the Talmud 'throws out' (i.e., advances) two equally authoritative and seemingly contradictory statements, one against the other, in order to clarify their meanings. The term is applied only in the case of conflicting mishnayos or *baraisos.* Similarly, when two contradictory Scriptural verses are advanced for clarification, the *Gemara* states: רָמֵי קְרָאֵי אַהֲדָדֵי. In *Bava Metzia* (71a), when the interpretation of a verse is challenged with a mishnah, the term וּרְמִינְהוּ is employed.

(29) וְתַנָּא תּוּנָא, *the Tanna teaches:* The present *Tanna* supports this argument.

(30) זוֹ (וְאֵינוֹ צָרִיךְ לוֹמַר) זוֹ, זוֹ ואצ״ל זוֹ, *this and of course that:* This expression informs us that the law contained in the first part of the mishnah is more innovative than that contained in the second. When a mishnah contains four or more parts, the *Tanna* will never arrange two in a לֹא זוֹ אַף זוֹ (see §34) pattern and the other two in a זוֹ ואצ״ל זוֹ pattern. When the *Gemara,* in answer to a difficulty, offers that the *Tanna's* method of teaching was זוֹ ואצ״ל זוֹ, it does so only as a last resort.

(31) חַסּוּרֵי מִיחַסְּרָא, *there is an omission:* This expression indicates that the omission is total, that not even an allusion to the missing section exists in the remaining statement.

(32) יֵשׁ אוֹמְרִים, *some say:* This refers to R' Nassan. אֲחֵרִים אוֹמְרִים, *others say,* refers to R' Meir. [This rule applies only in the majority of cases.]

(33) כִּבְיָכוֹל — That is, the Torah — which was written with כ״ב,

twenty-two, letters — יְכוֹלָה, *could have* said this, but not we. Others consider the word an acronym for כָּתוּב בַּתּוֹרָה, *it is written in the Torah*, related to the teaching: *If it were not actually written in Scripture, it would not be possible* (יָכוֹל) *to say such a thing. Rashi* (*Yoma* 3b) explains that this term means, *as if it were possible to say so*. Thus, according to *Rashi*, the word would be pronounced כִּבְיָכוֹל *(Shelah).*

(34) לֹא זוֹ אַף זוֹ, *not just this, but even that:* This expression informs us that the law in the second part of the mishnah is more novel than the one taught in the first part. Indeed, Rabbi could have inserted only the second law, from which the first would have been inferred; however, the *Tanna* characteristically may choose to introduce the less novel idea first, and then proceed to teach the more innovative halachah. Also, וְכֵן is, for the most part, synonymous with לֹא זוֹ אַף זוֹ. The לֹא זוֹ אַף זוֹ term is used only when the second halachah subsumes the first.

(35) לֵימָא הַנֵּי תַּנָּאֵי כְּהַנֵּי תַּנָּאֵי, *say that the dispute between these Tannaim is identical to the dispute between those other Tannaim:* The *Gemara* makes this statement because it is bothered that the same controversy is reported twice, only worded differently in each case. Further, the author of the mishnah or *baraisa* should have combined the pairs of disputing *Tannaim* into one mishnah, as follows: *Rabbi ... and Rabbi ... both say ...*

(36) לֵימָא כְּתַנָּאֵי, *shall we say it involves a dispute between Tannaim?:* That is, do we say that *Tannaim* argue about the matter discussed by that *Amora*, or the controversy between these two *Amoraim?* On the contrary, since the *Amora* came to state the law, he should have done so in the name of the appropriate *Tanna;* and since he stated it anonymously, apparently all the *Tannaim* agree to it. Where the Talmud acknowledges that the matter does involve a dispute between *Tannaim*, it states: כְּתַנָּאֵי (it is a dispute between *Tannaim)* — without לֵימָא.

(37) לֵימָא מְסַיֵּיעַ לֵיהּ, *say that it supports him:* A supporting statement or proof is adduced to corroborate the opinion of an *Amora*.

(38) מַאי בֵּינַיְיהוּ, *what is the difference between them?* When two sages arrive at the same legal opinion, yet for completely

different reasons, the *Gemara* seeks to know why they disagree in the theory.

(39) מַאי קמ״ל (קָא מַשְׁמַע לָן)? תְּנֵינָא!, *What is he telling us? We have already learnt it!:* This question is asked when the reference is to an explicit teaching in the Mishnah. אַף אֲנַן נַמִּי תְּנֵינָא, *we too have learnt it:* The question is phrased thus when the teaching comes only from an inference.

(40) מְגַדֵּף בָּהּ: Synonymous with מַתְקִיף לָהּ, *So-and so demurred.*

(41) מֵימְרָא, *dictum:* Even though a dictum cites a *Tanna* as its source (i.e., 'Rabbi ... said in the name of a certain *Tanna'),* the Talmud does not use the phrase מֵיתֵיבֵי when bringing the dictum to challenge another opinion, since the statement is essentially a quote and does not have the status of a *baraisa.*

(42) מַכְרִיעַ, *determinant:* When two sages are in disagreement and a third sides with one of them — even on only one point while disputing the others — he is called *the determinant,* and the halachah follows his opinion. However, when the third sage renders an altogether different opinion than the other two, he is called a *third determinant,* and the halachah does not follow him. (However, there are several other versions of this rule.)

(43) סְבָרָא, *logical argument:* It is important to note that the logical arguments of the Sages are an authentic part of the Oral Law that Moses received at Sinai, and that all the laws based on such arguments are considered actual Torah. The Talmud's statement at the beginning of *Zevachim* (2a) — *If you like I shall offer* [*as proof*] *a logical argument, and if you like I shall cite Scripture* — indicates the parity between such an argument and Scripture, for indeed any Torah truth that comes from the human intellect is considered as though it was derived from the Written Law. In fact, the Talmud (see *Kesubos* 22a, *Bava Kamma* 46b) often wonders: *Why do we need a Scriptural verse* [*as a source*]? *It can be deduced from logic!* However, instances occur in the Talmud when both logic and Scripture are equally possible, yet the *Gemara* fails to ask why the verse is needed (as above). *Tosafos* (*Shevuos* 22b) explain that in such cases the logical argument is particularly complex, and the verse is needed to clarify the logic.

(44) סוּגְיָא, *a Talmudic passage:* The term literally means the *walk* and *path* of the Talmud. For this reason Jewish Law is called

הֲלָכָה, from הִילּוּךְ, *walk* (i.e., it elucidates the direction that the Jew must walk in life).

(45) צְרִיכוּתָא: This establishes the necessity of two separate matters, and that one could not have been derived from the other. The actual expression as it appears in the *Gemara:* צְרִיכָא, *it is needed.*

(46) קַשְׁיָא, *it is difficult:* Whenever a statement in the Talmud is challenged, and the *Gemara* concludes with this expression, the original statement is not invalidated, but remains extant with an unresolved difficulty. *Ritva (to Bava Basra* 52b) writes about one of the sages of Provence who provided answers for all such unresolved questions in the Talmud. *Rashbam* (*Bava Basra* 52b) disputes this.

קַשְׁיָא לְהוּ, *they found it difficult;* קַשְׁיָא לֵיהּ, *he found it difficult:* Whenever two questions are posed, and the second is prefaced by וְעוֹד, *and further,* the second question is necessarily related to and stronger than the first.

(47) רַבָּנָן דְּבֵי רַב, *the students of the yeshivah:* בֵּי רַב does not mean the School of Rav, but refers to any Torah academy. אָמְרֵי בֵּי רַב, *the School of Rav say:* In the majority of cases this expression actually refers to the School of Rav.

(48) שִׁיטָה, *opinion:* The inferred consensus of a group of sages based on an analysis of their individual views on diverse topics. This usually appears in the form: *R' ..., R' ..., and R' ... all hold that ...* The halachah does not follow the opinion of a *shitah. Rabbeinu Tam* disputes this, however.

(49) שְׁמַע מִינָּה, *infer it:* Repetition of this expression signifies the conclusion of the Talmudic dialectic, but if it is stated only once no conclusion has yet been reached.

(50) תָּא שְׁמַע, *come, listen (and I will answer your question):* Sometimes this expression means: *Come, listen (and I shall ask you a question).*

(51) תְּיוּבְתָּא, *a response, retort:* An *Amora's* statement has been successfully challenged.

מֵיתִיבֵי: When the *Gemara* questions an *Amora* from the evidence of a *baraisa,* it uses a derivate of the word תְּיוּבְתָּא, which means *response* or *retort.* Hence, when several sages are asking, the term used is מֵיתִיבֵי; when the question comes from an individual, the expression is אֵיתִיבֵיהּ or מָתִיב.[3]

(52) תֵּיקוּ, *it stands over:* This term derives from תֵּיקוּם, *let it stand,* indicating that the question still stands and the matter remains in doubt. Others suggest that the four letters form an acronym for: תִּשְׁבִּי יְתָרֵץ קוּשְׁיוֹת וְאִבָּעְיוֹת, *Tishbi* (the prophet Elijah, a native of Toshav) *will resolve all the difficulties and questions.*[4]

(53) תְּנָא, *it was taught;* תְּנָא עֲלָהּ, *It was taught on it:* These terms introduce a *tosefta,* which supplements the teachings of the Mishnah.

(54) תָּנוּ רַבָּנָן, *the Rabbis have taught:* This refers to a *baraisa* that was familiar to all.

(55) תָּנֵי חֲדָא, *one taught;* תַּנְיָא אִידָךְ, *the other taught;* תַּנְיָא, *it was taught:* These terms all refer to a *baraisa.*

(56) תְּנַן, *we have learned in a mishnah.* However, there are occasional instances when this expression refers to a *baraisa.* The term always introduces a question.

(57) תְּנַן הָתָם, *we learned in a mishnah found in another tractate* (lit.,

---

3. The Talmud does not refute one *Amora* with a statement of another *Amora* (hence the expression גַּבְרָא אַגַּבְרָא קָרָמֵית?, *you are challenging one man's opinion because of another's?),* with the exception of Rav, whose opinions are cited to refute the statements of *Amoraim* who came after him.

Rashi writes that Rabbah was an important man, and the *Gemara,* when objecting, cites his opinions or Rav's as if they were stated in a mishnah or *baraisa* (*Rashi* to *Bava Kamma* 33b, s.v. הא). *Tosafos* (*Moed Kattan* 2b) write that it is possible to use the opinions of R' Kahana to refute Rabbah and R' Yosef, because R' Kahana was a great man whose intellect was exceedingly sharp. Likewise, it is permissible to cite the opinions of *Amoraim* (to refute others) when it has been determined that they represent the halachah.

4. I have heard the following question asked: Why, with regard to lost items which are not claimed by their owners, does the *Gemara* say: *Let it remain here until Elijah comes (Bava Metzia* 3a), while with regard to uncertainties in the Halachah, the *Gemara* states that *Tishbi will resolve* and not that *Elijah will resolve?*

The answer lies in the fact that Elijah, in addition to being a prophet, was also a great sage, actually enumerated as one of the receivers of the Torah. Therefore, we do not require Elijah acting in the capacity of prophet to unravel the mysteries of the Halachah, for the Torah *is not in the heavens (Deut.* 30:12). Rather, we await his imminent return in the role of sage, when he will restore the Torah to us in its entirety, thereby revitalizing the Tradition; hence, we refer to him in this aspect of his mission as *Tishbi,* the sage from Toshav, his place of residence, and not as Elijah the Prophet. However, with regard to unclaimed lost articles, we proclaim: *Let it remain here until Elijah comes,* for through his supernatural power of prophecy he will reveal the particulars of true ownership.

there). However, sometimes the Talmud merely writes תְּנַן without adding הָתָם, though the reference is to a mishnah in another tractate. This expression introduces a new subject of discussion.

(58) תִּסְתַּיֵּים, *it can be concluded:* This expression is used when the *Gemara* wants to prove something that was hitherto unknown to us. When תִּסְתַּיֵּים is written twice, such is the conclusion of the *Gemara.*

(59) תָּפַסְתָּ מְרוּבָּה לֹא תָּפַסְתָּ, תָּפַסְתָּ מִיעוּטָא תָּפַסְתָּ, *if you grasp much you have not grasped, if you grasp little, you have grasped:* When a novel interpretation is inferred from a superfluous word or phrase in a mishnah, only its narrowest definition is accepted.

(60) תִּפְשׁוֹט מֵהָא, *resolve it from this:* Answer the difficulty from a *baraisa.* תִּפְשׁוֹט מֵהָכָא, *resolve it from here* — from the teaching currently being discussed.

(61) תַּקָּנָה, *regulation:* Some hold that every anonymous regulation was promulgated in Ezra's court.

Addendum:
הֲלָכָה לְמֹשֶׁה מִסִּינַי
A Tradition Received by Moses at Sinai

The commandment of *tefillin* (phylacteries) encompasses three distinct categories of laws, and a closer study of them will illustrate our point well. The Torah itself states: *Bind them as a sign on your arm, and let them be* totafos (טֹטָפֹת) *between your eyes (Deut.* 6:8). The Torah explictly commands us to wear *tefillin* on the arm and between the eyes, yet leaves unclear the meaning of *totafos.* The Torah also does not specify the exact number of passages which must be written on parchment and inserted into the boxes. However, our Sages received a tradition from Sinai regarding the identity and number of passages to be written, and found support for the Oral Tradition from the language of Scripture itself: The word *totafos* implies four (passages) — *tot,* which means *two* in *Katpi* (a certain language), and *fos,* which means two in *Afriki* (a language of North Africa) *(Sanhedrin* 4b). Thus, even though the Sages learned the number of passages from a tradition originating at Sinai, since they found support for it in Scripture this law cannot be considered a הֲלָכָה לְמֹשֶׁה מִסִּינַי, *a tradition received by Moses at Sinai.*

Others laws of *tefillin* were derived using the rules of Biblical exegesis. For instance, Abaye learned from a *gezeirah shavah* (see page 129) that *between your eyes* actually means that the head-*tefillin* should be placed on the hair *(Kiddushin* 36a). That the other phylactery should be bound to the *left* arm is derived from the Torah's writing יָדְכָה, *your arm,* with the letter *he* at the end of the word, from which the Sages interpreted that the weak arm was intended *(Menachos* 37a).

That the parchment used for the *tefillin* should not come from an impure animal is also learned from a Scriptural interpretation: *So that Hashem's Torah may be in your mouth (Ex.* 13:7), i.e., the parchment should come from that which is permitted to be put in your mouth: ritually pure animals *(Shabbos* 108a). These laws, which are derived from Scriptural exegesis, also cannot be considered a tradition received by Moses at Sinai.

However, in the laws of *tefillin* there are ten halachos which are impossible to extract from the Written Torah: (a) The passages must be written with black ink; (b) they must be written on parchment that comes from the outer side of the animal's inner skin; (c) the boxes and the stitching should be squared; (d) the phylactery worn on the head should bear the form of the letter *shin* on both the left and right sides of the box; (e) the passages should be wrapped with animal skin; (f) they should also be wrapped with animal hair; (g) the boxes should be sewn shut with thread made from an animal's sinew; (h) there should be an opening along the side of the box for the strap to pass through; (i) the straps should be painted black; (j) the strap of the phylactery worn on the arm should be knotted in such a way as to form the letter *dalet.* These ten laws are all traditions received by Moses at Sinai.

Rambam (Introduction to Mishnah Commentary of Seder Zeraim) writes on this topic:

> Even though certain laws were received directly from Moses, we cannot call them traditions received by Moses at Sinai. For we cannot say that the identification of פְּרִי עֵץ הָדָר, *the fruit of the beautiful tree (Lev.* 23:40) as an *esrog*/citron, or the obligation of one who intentionally strikes another to pay damages, should be considered in this category, since we have

already explained that these interpretations were taught by Moses and are alluded to in Scripture, or were logically explicated from Scripture, and only those laws which are not hinted at in the Written Torah and have no basis therein, and which may not be logically extrapolated therefrom, may be called traditions received by Moses at Sinai.

Thus, when we said that all halachic measurements were in this category *(Eruvin* 14a; see *Hagahos R' Mattisyahu Strashun* ibid.), they asked us, 'Why do you say this? Certainly, the measurements are implied in Scripture, in the verse *(Deut.* 8:8): ... אֶרֶץ חִטָּה וּשְׂעֹרָה, *A land of wheat and barley ...'* To this we can answer that there are means of deriving them logically or by inference from Scripture; rather, the Rabbis identified each measurement with an appropriate verse as a mnemonic device by which they might be learned and remembered ... and this is what is meant whenever the Talmud says, *'The verse is only an* אַסְמַכְתָּא, *support.'*

However, *Ritva's* view of אַסְמַכְתָּא is diametrically opposed to that of *Rambam.* He writes in *Rosh Hashanah* (16a, s.v. תניא):

> Any oral law for which there is a support in the Torah is not actually a Scriptural obligation, but only an indication from God of something that is proper to do. However, the Sages were given the authority to establish it as an obligation. This explanation is unequivocal and true, unlike those of other commentators who maintain that the support is only a mnemonic aid given by the Sages, and not the actual intent of the Torah, God forbid. Perish the thought, for such an opinion amounts to heresy. Rather, a support means that the Torah intimated as such, and gave the Sages the authority to establish the matter as law if they so chose, as it is written *(Deut.* 17:10), *And you shall do according to the thing that they shall tell you.* Thus, you will find that the Sages invariably adduce a proof or hint or support from the Torah, indicating that no law is initiated solely by them. Indeed, the entire Oral Law is alluded to in the Written Law, which itself is perfect, lacking nothing, God forbid.

Rambam (Hil. Mamrim 1:2) writes that the Sanhedrin used to establish and decide the law in one of two ways: (a) through Biblical exegesis, using the thirteen hermeneutical rules (see ch. 13); (b) from tradition received by Moses at Sinai. For the Torah states *(Deut.*

17:11): *And regarding the law that they shall say,* referring to law derived with the Thirteen Rules, and *from everything that they shall tell you* (ibid.), which means the tradition that was transmitted through the generations. The difference between the two methods of adjudication is as follows: If the law was determined hermeneutically, then a subsequent body of the Sanhedrin may render a different interpretation. But if Sanhedrin once established a law as tradition received by Moses, others can never subsequently overturn that decision, inasmuch as it is an authentic tradition from Sinai. For there is no controversy regarding the tradition, and so the incidence of a dispute over a law indicates that the law never originated with Moses.

Chapter Eleven
Select Bibliography of Works of Chazal

*This bibliography only lists works composed before the sealing of the Talmud. Many holy books, on both the revealed and hidden parts of the Torah, are not included in this list. In fact, only a small fraction are mentioned here. (b) Works no longer extant are marked with an asterisk.**

Books on the Revealed Torah

(1) *Aggadas Bereishis*
(2) *Osiyos d'Rabbi Akiva*
(3) *Baraisa d'Shmuel Hakatan*
(4) *Baraisa d'Mazalos*
(5) *Baraisa d'Meleches Hamishkan*
(6) *Passover Haggadah*
(7) The seven small tractates:
- (a) *Sefer Torah*
- (b) *Tefillin*
- (c) *Tzitzis*
- (d) *Mezuzah*
- (e) *Kusim*
- (f) *Geirim*
- (g) *Avadim*

(8) The tractates:
- (a) *Avos d'Rabbi Nassan*
- (b) *Sofrim*
- (c) *Semachos*
- (d) *Kallah*

(e) *Derech Eretz*
(f) *Eretz Yisrael**
(g) *Perek Hashalom*
(9) *Midrash Rabbah* on the Pentateuch
(10) *Midrash* on the five *Megillos*
(11) *Midrash Zuta* on the five *Megillos*
(12) *Megillas Chassidim*
(13) *Megillas Taanis*
(14) *Mechilta d'Rabbi Yishmael*
(15) *Mechilta d'Rabbi Shimon bar Yochai*
(16) *Midrash Yelamdenu**
(17) *Midrash Tanchuma*
(18) *Midrash Konen*
(19) *Midrash Vayosha*
(20) *Midrash Aseres Hadibros*
(21) *Midrash Vayisau*
(22) *Midrash Tadshe*
(23) *Midrash Hallel*
(24) *Midrash Agur*
(25) *Midrash Avkir**
(26) *Midrash Mishlei*
(27) *Midrash Yonah*
(28) *Midrash Shocher Tov* on *Psalms*
(29) *Midrash Iyov* (Job)
(30) *Midrash Shmuel*
(31) *Midrash Vayechulu*
(32) *Midrash Esfah**
(33) *Midrash Abba Gurion*
(34) *Midrash Harninu**
(35) *Midrash Temurah*
(36) Tractate *Chibut Hakever*
(37) Tractate *Gehinnom* and *Pirkei Gan Eden*
(38) *The Book of Adam HaRishon**
(39) *Sefer Refuos** (Book of Cures) [*Chizkiyahu concealed it.*]
(40) *Sifra (Toras Kohanim)*
(41) *Sifrei* on *Numbers* and *Deuteronomy*
(42) *Sifrei Zuta*
(43) *Seder Olam*
(44) *Sefer Hayashar*

(45) *Pirkei d'Rabbi Eliezer*
(46) *Pesikta Rabbasi*
(47) *Pesikta d'Rav Kahana*
(48) *Perek Shirah*
(49) *Pirkei Eliyahu*
(50) The Six Orders of the *Mishnah*
(51) *Targum Yonasan ben Uziel* on the Prophets
(52) *Targum Kesuvim* (Hagiographa)
(53) *Targum R' Yosef* on *Chronicles*
(54) *Targum Onkelos* on the Torah
(55) *Targum Yerushalmi* on the Torah
(56) *Targum Yonasan* on the Torah
(57) *Targum Chamesh* (The Five) *Megillos*
(58) *Tosefta*
(59) *Talmud Yerushalmi* (Jerusalem Talmud)
(60) *Talmud Bavli* (Babylonian Talmud)
(61) *Tanna d'bei Eliyahu*

Books on the Secrets of the Torah

(1) *Idra Rabba* and *Zutra*
(2) *Zohar* on the Pentateuch
(3) *Zohar Chadash*
(4) Tractate *Atzilus*
(5) *Midrash Mei HaShilu'ach*
(6) *Midrash Hane'elam*
(7) *Sifra d'Chanoch**
(8) *Sifra d'Adam Kadmaah**
(9) *Sefer Habahir*
(10) *Sifra d'Rav Yaiva Sabbah**
(11) *Sifra d'Rav Yaisa Sabbah**
(12) *Sifra d'Rabbi Krospadai Chamid Liba**
(13) *Sifra d'Tzeniusa*
(14) *Sifra d'Rav Hamnunah Sabbah**
(15) *Sefer Yetzirah*
(16) *Sisrei Torah*
(17) *Pirkei Heichalos*
(18) *Tikuni Zohar*

The *gaon,* R' Avraham, son of the *Vilna Gaon,* writes in his introduction to *Sefer Aggadas Bereishis:* It is written in the *Yayin Harokeach* by R' Elazar of Worms that in the verse *(Song of Songs* 6:8), *There are sixty queens ..., queens* refers to the sixty tractates of the Talmud, the *eighty concubines* represent the eighty *Midrashim,* and *maidens without number* refers to the *baraisos* dealing with Creation and the מַעֲשֵׂה מֶרְכָּבָה, *vision of the Divine Chariot.* In *Tikunim* (p. 143) it states that the *eighty concubines* symbolize the eighty works of *Aggadah,* and that *maidens* refers to the halachos, which are innumerable.

Chapter Twelve
Weights, Measures and Currency

[Editor's note: For the reader's convenience we have provided approximate U.S. equivalents for the weights and measures. Authorities differ widely regarding these equivalencies. Those given before the slash are based upon the calculations of the *Chazon Ish,* while those after the slash are based upon the ruling of Rabbi Avraham Chaim Noeh's *Shiurei Torah.* The figures of authorities whose calculations do not coincide with either of these two almost always lie somewhere between them.]

Measures of Distance

(1) טֶפַח, *tefach* [pl. *tefachim*] (handbreadth): the width of 4 thumbs, 5 middle fingers, or 6 small fingers[1] [3.8 / *3.2* inches]
(2) זֶרֶת, *zeres* (span): 3 *tefachim* [11.35 / *9.5* inches]
(3) אַמָּה, *ammah* [pl. *ammos*] (cubit): 6 *tefachin* [22.8 / *18.9* inches]
(4) רִיס, *ris:* 266 2/3 *ammos* [168.1 / *126* yards]
(5) מִיל, *mil:* 2000 *ammos*, or 7½ *ris;* this distance is also known as a תְחוּם שַׁבָּת, *Sabbath boundary*[2] [1269 / *1028* yards]
(6) פַּרְסָה, *parsah (Persian mile):* 4 *mil* [2.9 / *2.3* miles]
(7) מַהֲלַךְ יוֹם, *a day's walk: 10 parsah* [29 / *23* miles]

---

1. Measurement is made at the widest part of the thumb — at the joint — of an average-sized man. A *tefach* is also equivalent to the width of seven average kernels of barley laid side by side.

2. [On the Sabbath or festivals a person is forbidden to go more than this distance from what was his halachically defined place of dwelling at the onset of that day (see ArtScroll *Eruvin,* p. 10.).]

Measures of Volume

[Editor's note: Most of the measures in this section are based upon the volume of an egg (Hebrew בֵּיצָה, *beitzah;* Aramaic בֵּיעָא, *bei'a)* equivalent to approximately 3.5 / *2* fluid ounces.]

(1) כַּזַּיִת, *kazayis* (the size of an olive): There are two opinions — (a) ½ egg [1.7 / *1* fluid ounce]; or (b) ⅓ egg [1.2 / *.67* fl. oz.]
(2) כֹּתֶבֶת, *koseves:* slightly less than one egg
(3) רְבִיעִית, *reviis (¼ log):* 1.5 eggs [5.3 / *3* fluid ounces]
(4) פְּרָס, *peras:* There are two opinions — (a) 4 eggs, or (b) 3 eggs[3]
(5) לֹג, *log* [Aramaic, לֻגָּא, *luga,* pl. *lugin*]: 6 eggs[4] [21.2 / *12* fl. oz.]
(6) רוֹבַע, *rova;* 6 eggs[4] [21.2 / *12* fluid ounces]
(7) קַב, *kav* [pl. *kabim*]: 4 *lugin* [2.65 / *1.5* quarts]
(8) תַּרְקַב, *tarkav:* 3 *kabim* [8 / *4.5* quarts]
(9) סְאָה, *se'ah* [pl. *se'in*]: 6 *kabim* [4 / *2.25* gallons]
(10) אֵיפָה, *ephah* [pl. *ephos*]: 3 *se'in*[5] [12 / *6.75* gallons]
(11) לֶתֶךְ, *lesech:* 5 *ephos* [60 / *33.75* gallons]
(12) כּוֹר, *kor:* 10 *ephos,* or 30 *se'in* [120 / *67.5* gallons]

Measures of Surface Area

(1) עֲדָשָׁה, *adashah* (lentil): 4 grains of barley[6]
(2) גְּרִיס, *gris* (bean): 9 lentils, or 36 grains of barley
(3) בֵּית סְאָה, *beis*[7] *se'ah:* 2500 square *ammos* [1003 / *689* square yards]
(4) בֵּית סָאתַיִם, *beis*[7] *sasaim*: 5000 square *ammos* [2006 / *1378* square yards]

---

3. [This measurement is used to determine the period known as כְּדֵי אֲכִילַת פְּרָס, *the time it takes to eat a piece,* i.e., a piece of bread with the volume of 3 or 4 eggs. Opinions regarding the amount of time involved range between 2 and 9 minutes.]

4. [The term *log* is usually used with liquids, while *rova* is used as a dry measure. Their volumes are identical — 6 eggs.]

5. *Shelah* suggests the word גודו *(Daniel* 4:11) serves as a mnemonic to remember the measures of volume found in the Talmud: One *ephah is 3 se'in* (ג = 3); one *se'ah* is six *kabim* (ו = 6); one *kav* is four *lugin* (ד = 4); and one *log* is 6 eggs (ו = 6). [This is also attributed to *R' Bachya* in *Derushim Nechmadim* by *Maharam Shif,* printed after his commentary to *Chullin* in many editions of the Talmud.]

6. See *Negaim* 6:1.

7. [The word בֵּית, literally *house of,* refers to the area needed for the planting of a *se'ah/sasaim* (two *se'ah)/kor* of barley seeds.]

(5) בֵּית כּוֹר, *beis*[7] *kor:* 75,000 square *ammos*[8] [6.2 / 4.3 acres]

Weights

(1) פְּרוּטָה, *perutah:* ½ medium grain of barley [.386 grains]
(2) דִּינָר, *dinar:* 96 grains of barley [74.1 grains]
(3) תַּרְטֵימַר, *tarteimar:* 50 *dinarim* [8.5 ounces]
(4) (אִיטַלְקִי) מָנֶה, *(Italian) maneh:* 2 *tarteimar* [17 ounces]
(5) כִּכָּר, *kikar:* 60 (Italian) *maneh* [64 pounds]

Currency

(1) אִיסָּר, *issar:* 8 *perutos*
(2) פּוּנְדְיוֹן, *pundeyon:* 2 *issarim*
(3) מְעָה, *me'ah* [pl. *maos*]: 2 *pundeyonim*
(4) זוּז, *zuz*[9]: 6 *maos*
(5) סֶלַע, *sela*[10]: 4 *zuzim,* or 2 *shekalim,* or 24 *maos*[11]
(6) דִּינָר זָהָב, gold *dinar:* 25 *zuzim*
(7) מָנֶה, *maneh:* 100 *zuzim,* or 4 gold *dinars*

---

8. *Rashi* to *Kiddushin* 60b describes a square with sides that measures slightly more than 273.5 *ammos* and 2 *tefachim.*

9. The *zuz* and the silver *dinar* have the same value.

10. Another coin called סֶלַע מְדִינָה, *selah medinah,* is equal to half a *zuz.* [Generally, all Biblical obligations are computed in כֶּסֶף צוֹרִי, *Tyrian silver,* while Rabbinical obligations are reckoned in כֶּסֶף מְדִינָה, *provincial silver,* an alloy of one-part silver to seven parts copper. Tyrian silver was valued at eight times as much as provincial silver.]

11. Some suggest the word דּוֹבֵב *(Song of Songs* 7:10) as a mnemonic device for remembering these figures: one *sela* is four *zuzim* (ד = 4); one *zuz* is six *maos* (ו = 6); one *me'ah* equals two *pundeyonim* (ב = 2); and one *pundeyon* equals two *issarim* (ב = 2) *(Maharam Shif,* citing *R' Bachya,* loc. cit.).

Chapter Thirteen
The Thirteen Rules of Biblical Exegesis

It is important to understand that we are no longer empowered to interpret the Written Torah using any of the thirteen rules of exegesis (*Maharik* Shoresh 139; *Ra'ah* to *Kesubos* cited in *Yad Malachi* 144). *Bach (Choshen Mishpat* 289), upon discovering a Scriptural interpretation offered by *Tur* that seemingly was never mentioned in the Talmud, exclaims: *It is impossible that* Tur *would make an original interpretation of Scripture, one found neither in the Mishnah nor the Talmud!* He subsequently labored diligently to uncover a Talmudic source for *Tur's* interpretation. *R' Eliyahu Mizrachi* (*Numbers* 30:2) is amazed that *Rashi* initiates such an interpretation[1]: 'I do not understand how *Rashi* made this interpretation, since only the Sages of the Mishnah, who received these explanations as traditions, are authorized to do so and no one else, not even the early *Geonim*, and certainly not their successors.'

From the above it is clear that we seek knowledge of the rules of exegesis only in order to understand how our Sages interpreted Scripture, but not to apply them ourselves.

The Thirteen Hermeneutic Rules are called מִדּוֹת, *measures*, since before employing any one of them the Sages had to 'measure' a number of factors — how, under which conditions, and when to use them (*Netziv*, Introduction to *Haamek She'elah* on *Sheiltos*).

---

1. *Rashi* makes an אִם אֵינוֹ עִנְיָן, *if it does not apply*, interpretation, which works as follows: If the Torah indicates a halachah in a case or category where it is already known, then apply that halachah to another situation.

I

קַל וָחֹמֶר / Kal Vachomer

(The A Fortiori Argument)

In this interpretation, inference of a stringency is drawn from a lenient case (*kal*) to a strict one (*chomer*), and inference of a leniency is drawn from a strict case to a lenient one. The logic is compelling: If the more lenient case contains a particular stringency, then all the more so should the stricter case. And conversely, if the stricter case contains a particular leniency, then certainly the more lenient case should have it too.

Ten examples of this rule are explicitly mentioned in the Torah. According to R' Yishmael, cited in *Bereishis Rabbah* 92, they are:

1) Upon being accused of stealing Joseph's goblet, the brothers replied, *Here look: the money that we found in the mouth of our sacks we brought back to you from the land of Canaan. How, then, could we have stolen from your master's house any silver or gold? (Gen.* 44:8).

(2) Upon being told by God to order Pharaoh to release the Jews, Moses responded: *Behold, the children of Israel have not listened to me; how, then, shall Pharaoh listen to me? (Ex.* 6:12).

(3) Explaining why Miriam must be banished from the camp for speaking *lashon hara* (evil gossip), as a result of which she was stricken with leprosy, God told Moses: *If her father had but spit in her face, should she not be ashamed seven days?* Then, certainly, *Let her be shut out from the camp seven days,* away from the Divine Presence (*Num.* 12:14).

(4) Moses chastised the Jews before his death: *Behold, while I am alive with you this day, you have been rebellious against* HASHEM*; and how much more so after my death? (Deut.* 31:27).

(5) God, demanding faith and patience of Jeremiah: *If you have run with the footmen and they have wearied you, how, then, can you contend with horses? (Jer.* 12:5).

(6) *And in a land of peace where you are secure, how will you do in the thickets of the Jordan?* (ibid.).

(7) King David's soldiers expressing their apprehension over the prospect of fighting the Philistines far from their home: *Behold, we are afraid here in Judah; how much more so if we go to Ke'ilah against the armies of the Philistines? (I Sam.* 23:3).

(8) Regarding punishment for sin during man's earthly existence: *Behold, the righteous shall be repaid on the earth; how much more the wicked and the sinner! (Proverbs* 11:31).

(9) King Ahaseurus reporting the casualty figures to Queen Esther: *In Shushan the capital, the Jews have slain and annihilated five hundred men, as well as the sons of Haman. What must they have done in the rest of the King's provinces! (Esther* 9:12).

(10) Comparing sinful Israel to a degenerate vine that has become valueless, and further has been reduced to a mere fragment by the loss of the Ten Tribes, the prophet seeks to justify the impending national catastrophe: *Behold, when it was whole, it was fit for no work; how much less, when the fire has consumed it and it is singed, shall it be fit for any work? (Ezekiel* 15:5).

Stringent or Lenient?

The factors that determine whether a case is considered stringent or lenient fall into two categories: (a) logic; (b) the laws of the Torah that pertain to the case.

An example of the first group would be: If one is liable for the damages caused by his animal when it did not intend any harm, then, certainly, he should be liable for damages which the animals did intend to inflict (*Bava Kamma* 4b).

An example of the latter category: If a Jewish bondwoman, who cannot be acquired by an act of cohabitation, can be bought with money, then a wife, who may be acquired [for קִידּוּשִׁין, the first stage of marriage] through cohabitation,[2] may certainly be acquired with money (*Kiddushin* 4b).

Refuting a Kal Vachomer

The *kal vachomer* argument can be refuted with a *pircha* (rebuttal) in one of two ways: (a) challenging the origin of the *kal*

---

2. [This is true only according to Biblical law; the Rabbis, however, subsequently forbade use of this method.]

vachomer itself; (b) challenging the conclusion by bringing proof to the contrary from a third case.

In the first category, the refutation is based on the case from which we wish to infer the *kal vachomer*. That is, if we want to apply a particular stringency of a lenient case to a stricter case, and we discover another stringency in the former that is not found in the latter, the *kal vachomer* is refuted because we have undermined its very starting point. For we can argue as follows: just as there is another stringency that exists in the lenient case and is not found in the stricter case, we can assume that the stringency we had wished to apply likewise exists only in the lenient case.

Alternatively, the rationale of the *pircha* may be: perhaps the second stringency we just discovered is more severe than the first, and in fact caused the other stringency in the case we thought to be lenient, and actually that case is not more lenient than the other case. According to this explanation, the refutation tells us that there is no *kal vachomer* at all!

The second method of refuting a *kal vachomer* is by proof from a third case, which also has the stringency of the stricter case, but not the stringency of the lenient case. This demonstrates that although a case has the former stringency it does not necessarily have the latter stringency as well. For example, this type of refutation can be used against the *kal vachomer* mentioned above which reasons that if a Jewish bondwoman, who cannot be acquired by an act of cohabitation, may, however, be acquired with money, then a wife, who may be acquired through cohabitation, may certainly be acquired with money. The rebuttal would be brought from the case of the *yevamah* [the widow of one's childless brother[3]], who can be acquired by an act of cohabitation, but not with money (ibid.).

A refutation of the first type, in which the rebuttal is based on the case from which we wish to make the inference, can also be used against this same *kal vachomer*. The case of the Jewish bondwoman has a stringency which the case of the wife definitely lacks: the bondwoman may gain her release through a monetary payment,

3. [When a man dies childless, the Torah (*Deut.* 25:5-10) commands his paternal brother to marry his widow. This marriage is known as *yibum;* the brother, as the *yavam;* the widow, as the *yevamah.* The Torah also provides a mechanism, known as *chalitzah,* by which the widow can be released from her attachment to the brother (see *Deut.* 25:5*ff.* and General Introduction to ArtScroll *Yevamos*).]

something the wife cannot do. Therefore, perhaps the same is true regarding the ability to be acquired with money: it is applicable only to a bondwoman, but not a wife.

Refuting the Origin

A refutation of the origin of a *kal vachomer* may be adduced only from a stringency or leniency that is expressly attributed to the case by the Torah itself. However, considering a case stringent or lenient based on logic cannot serve this purpose, since it is possible to subsume the rebuttal itself into the *kal vachomer*.

For instance, in *Bava Kamma* (25a) a *kal vachomer* is advanced to prove that when one's animal causes the type of damage called קֶרֶן, *keren*,[4] to another person on the latter's property, the owner of the animal is fully liable. The *Gemara* reasons: If one's animal causes the types of damage known as שֵׁן, *shen*, and רֶגֶל, *regel*, to another person on public property, the owner of the animal is not liable, and yet, if the damage is committed on the other person's property, the animal's owner is fully liable. Surely, then, *keren*, for which the animal's owner is liable even if it occurred on public property, should entail full liability if it occurred on the other person's property.

Even though a refutation of the *kal vachomer* may be made — *shen* and *regel* possess a stringent factor not found in *keren*: that they are common types of injury, whereas the incidence of *keren* is infrequent — nevertheless, we can introduce this stringency into the *kal vachomer* itself, as follows: If *shen* and *regel*, which — despite the fact that they occur frequently do not make the owner liable when they are committed on public property — do incur full liability if done in the property of the damagee, then certainly *keren* — for which there is liability when committed on public property — should require the payment of full damages when occurring on the damagee's property. Thus we see that *keren* is not weakened by its lacking the stringent factor of *shen* and *regel* (their being a common tort), inasmuch as that factor did not increase the liability of *shen*

4. [*Keren* (horn) is an intentional, tortious act, such as goring, kicking or biting, on the part of one's animal. *Shen* (tooth) and *regel* (foot) are unintentional acts of harm done by the animal. *Shen* is a concomitant of an act of self-gratification, while *regel* is inflicted during ordinary ambulatory movement (see ArtScroll commentary to *Bava Kamma* 1:1).]

and *regel* in the public domain; hence, like any refutation based on logic, it cannot rebut a *kal vachomer*. However, any lenient or stringent feature expressed in the Torah regarding a case from which we wish to make the inference may be used to refute a *kal vachomer*. Since the Torah vested the 'lenient' case with such-and-such a stringency, it is possible to conclude that the case is actually the stricter of the two. Or, we may conclude that the stringency being used for refutation actually led to the existence of the original stringency in the 'lenient' case.

Rebutting the Refutation

It is possible to rebut a refutation of the origin of a *kal vachomer* by bringing proof from a third case upon which the refutation was based, and which nevertheless contains the first stringency of the lenient case that we wanted to apply to the stricter premise. This third case clearly demonstrates that the second stringency did not cause the existence of the first stringency in the lenient case; hence, the *kal vachomer* is in force.

However, this third case, which disproves the refutation, may itself be rebutted, thereby refuting the *kal vachomer*, if it possesses any feature not found in the stricter case (to which we wished to learn). The reasoning goes like this: The third case has another stringency which accounts for its possessing the first stringency of the lenient case, whereas the 'stricter' case lacks this other stringency as well.

However, if the 'lenient' case also lacks this particular feature of the third case, then it is possible to say that that factor is not responsible for the third case's possessing the first stringency of the lenient case, inasmuch as the latter has the first stringency without having the attribute of the third case. Hence, the refutation of the *kal vachomer* is indeed rebutted by this third case and the *kal vachomer* is valid.

An example of this entire process is found in *Kiddushin* (5b), where the *Gemara* seeks to prove that *chupah*,[5] which is effective for *nisuin* (the final stage of marriage), is also effective for *erusin*

---

5. [There is a controversy among the early authorities regarding the meaning of *chupah*. The most widely accepted method is to bring the couple under the bridal canopy (see General Introduction to ArtScroll *Kesubos* s.v. *Marriage*).]

(the first stage of marriage). The *Gemara* reasons: If a monetary payment — which is not effective as a means of *nisuin* — is an acceptable method of *erusin*, then surely *chupah* — which is effective for *nisuin* — is also an acceptable method of *erusin*. A refutation of the gist of the *kal vachomer* is then suggested: Money possesses a stringency not found in *chupah* — it can be used to redeem הֶקְדֵּשׁוֹת, *consecrated objects*, and מַעֲשֵׂר שֵׁנִי, *the second tithe.*

This refutation is then rebutted by bringing proof from a third case. Cohabitation is effective as a means of *erusin* even though it cannot redeem consecrated objects or the second tithe. Thus, we see that effecting *erusin* does not depend on having the capability to redeem holy objects.

This rebuttal is then disproved: since cohabitation can be used to acquire a *yevamah* (see above), it can therefore also be used to acquire a wife. Finally, the rebuttal of the refutation is upheld, based on the 'lenient' case, *money*. Although it is not an acceptable means of acquiring a *yevamah*, it can nevertheless be used for *erusin*. The refutation having been rebutted, the *kal vachomer* is valid once again.

צַד הַשָּׁוֶה / The Common Feature

When the *Gemara* reaches, during the course of the *kal vachomer* dialectic outlined above, the stages of the 'third-case disproof' and 'lenient-case disproof', it will then remark: *And thus the argument revolves — the distinguishing feature of one is not that of the other, nor is the distinguishing feature of this one that of the other; the* צַד הַשָּׁוֶה, *feature common to both ...* The intent is as follows: The refutation of the origin of the *kal vachomer* (i.e., of the lenient case) was rebutted by the third case. The refutation of the third case was then rebutted by the lenient case. The common factor of these two cases is that they both possess the feature that we originally wanted to apply to the 'stricter' case. With this 'common feature' reasoning, it is possible to accomplish the intended inference of the *kal vachomer*.

The commentators disagree on precisely how to define this common-feature' stage of the *kal vachomer* dialectic, discussed above. Some maintain that the Talmud is retreating from the *kal vachomer* mode of argument, and now essays a *binyan av* (see below) which consists of the 'common feature'. Other commentators hold, however, that the *kal vachomer* remains intact, because all the refutations against it have been eliminated; and since the lenient case remains a viable basis for a *kal vachomer*, the argument is still operative.

דַיּוֹ / Dayyo

The full force of the *kal vachomer* argument is qualified by a principle called דַיּוֹ, *dayyo* ('it is sufficient'). The complete Talmudic expression of the principle is : *It is quite sufficient if the law of the matter inferred is equivalent to that from which it is derived.* Simply put, this means that a *kal vachomer* can give the 'stricter' case only that degree of stringency found in the 'lenient' case — and no more (even though the 'stricter' case is in fact more strict than the minor premise). The principle of *dayyo* is derived from Scripture *(Num.* 12:14): *If her father had but spit in her face, should she not be ashamed seven days? Let her be shut out from the camp seven days ... And Miriam was shut out from the camp seven days.* (This is one of the ten *kal vachomer* arguments found in the Torah, see p. 121.) If for her father she should be ashamed seven days, then certainly in the case of Divine reproof she should be ashamed fourteen days! Yet, the number of days remains seven, for it is sufficient if the law of the matter inferred (the case of Divine reproof) be equivalent to that from which it is derived (the case of the father).

Application

The principle of *dayyo* is applied in two ways: (a) on the origin of the *kal vachomer* (i.e., the 'lenient' case), as illustrated above regarding Miriam's punishment; (b) on the conclusion of the *kal vachomer* (i.e., the 'stricter' case), and, specifically, on the stringency of the stricter case which allows us to learn from the lenient case. This means that the stringency which we wish to infer from the lenient case to the strict one cannot be more severe than the stringency of the strict case which initiated the *kal vachomer* in the first place, for without that original stringency we have no *kal vachomer*. Thus, that stringency is also perceived as an origin of the *kal vachomer*, upon which *dayyo* can be applied to limit the severity of the stricter case's newly acquired stringency to that of the old.

An example of *dayyo* applied to the stricter case is found regarding the *kal vachomer* discussed above (p. 124, from *Bava Kamma* 25a). If *shen* and *regel,* which cause no liability when committed on public property, nevertheless give rise to full liability if committed on the injured party's property, then *keren,* for which there is liability if it occurred on public property, certainly should cause full liability if committed on the property of the injured party. (In this example we cannot apply *dayyo* to the origin of the *kal vachomer* – requiring the stricter premise to be no more than the lenient case – since the lenient case is *shen* and *regel* in the injured party's property, and they do pay full damages.) Thus, we must apply *dayyo* to the conclusion of the *kal vachomer,* which is *keren's* own stringency that it creates liability on public property. Hence, it is sufficient for *keren* in the injured party's domain to be like *keren* in the public domain – in which case the owner pays only half the damages – since without the law of *keren* in the public domain there would be no *kal vachomer.*

There is a dispute in the *Gemara* (ibid.) between R' Tarfon and the Sages whether *dayyo* is applied if, by doing so, the *kal vachomer* will be entirely nullified. R' Tarfon holds that *dayyo* can work only when there is room for the *kal vachomer* as well, such as in the case of Miriam's confinement. There, the *kal vachomer* suggested that in the case of Divine reproof she should be ashamed for fourteen days. Subsequently, *dayyo* reduced the amount to seven, but still left room for the *kal vachomer* to operate, for without it we would not know the punishment for her case at all. However, in the example of *keren,* were we to apply *dayyo* the purpose of the *kal vachomer* would be defeated. For *dayyo* would limit *keren's* payment when committed in the private property of the injured party to that which it pays when done in public property – half the damages. Yet without this teaching of the *kal vachomer* we would know from Scripture that *keren* pays at least half the damages regardless of where it occurred. Therefore, R' Tarfon would hold that *dayyo* is not applicable in this situation, and thus *keren* would cause full liability when committed in the injured party's property, according to the unmodified *kal vachomer.* The Sages, on the other hand, maintain that *dayyo* can even nullify the *kal vachomer,* for that indeed is its strength. Their opinion is derived from the narrative of

Miriam's confinement, where it is twice written that she should be shut out of the camp for seven days. One mention in fact pronounces her punishment, while the second comes to eliminate the *kal vachomer* argument itself — that the punishment should extend for fourteen days. Thus, the Sages actually learn from Scripture that *dayyo* may defeat the *kal vachomer* completely.

No *kal vachomer* argument may involve a הֲלָכָה לְמשֶׁה מִסִּינַי, *a tradition received by Moses at Sinai,* since Moses was instructed that the rule of *kal vachomer* may be used to interpret only those laws expressly mentioned in the Written Torah. *Rashi* (*Shabbos* 132a) writes that a *kal vachomer* argument is not advanced from such a tradition, since the Oral Law cannot be interpreted with any of the thirteen hermeneutic rules. Certainly, a disproof of a refutation may not be drawn from them *(Rosh).*

אֵין מַזְהִירִין מִן הַדִּין — a novel prohibition derived by a *kal vachomer* argument lacks the stature of a prohibition mentioned in the Torah, and no corporal punishment is given for its violation. Likewise, אֵין עוֹנְשִׁין מִן הַדִּין — corporal punishment, even for violation of a prohibition mentioned in the Torah, cannot be inferred by a *kal vachomer.*

II

גְּזֵירָה שָׁוָה / Gezeirah Shavah

Two similar words which appear in two different places in the Torah are so written in order to infer from one to the other *(Halichos Olam).* This rule of interpretation is called *gezeirah shavah. Gezeirah* means *cut out,* implying a word which is 'cut out,' or distinguished, from the other words by the composition of its letters. *Shavah* (equal) refers to the similarity of the two words written in different passages *(R' Yosef Karo* in *Klalei HaGemara).*

Types of Inferences

Two types of inferences may be made through the rule of *gezeirah shavah:* (a) to explain or clarify what is already written in the Torah; (b) to derive a new law.

An example of a *gezeirah shavah* which provides an explanation: Regarding *erusin* (loosely, *betrothal),* it is stated *(Deut.* 22:13), *When a man takes* (יִקַּח) a wife; regarding the purchase of a field it is written *(Gen.* 23:13): *The price of the field — take* (קַח) *it from me.* The *gezeirah shavah,* which is derived from the two similar words for *taking* in the two disparate passages, teaches us that just as a field can be acquired by monetary payment, so too *erusin,* acquiring a wife, is accomplished with money (*Kiddushin* 2a).

A *gezeirah shavah* which teaches a new law: Regarding the Pesach offering the Torah speaks of a תּוֹשָׁב, *sojourner,* and a שָׂכִיר, *hired servant (Ex.* 12:45), and likewise in respect to *terumah,* the portion of the crop given to the *Kohen* (priest), it mentions a sojourner and a hired servant (*Lev.* 22:10). Hence, we derive that just as it is forbidden for the uncircumcised to partake of the Pesach offering, so, too, an uncircumcised *Kohen* may not eat *terumah* (*Yevamos* 70a).

Who May Formulate It

No sage may formulate a new *gezeirah shavah* on his own, but may use only those he received by tradition from his teacher, who received it from his teacher, all the way back in an unbroken chain of transmission to Moses, who received it from the Holy One at Sinai. This principle stands in contradistinction to the *kal vachomer,* which a sage can devise from his own reasoning. *Rashi* and *Tosafos* (*Sukkah* 31a) dispute whether novel interpretations may be made with the other hermeneutic rules, or whether there, too, such interpretations must be transmitted from master to disciple.

Types of Tradition

There are two types of tradition with respect to the *gezeirah shavah:* (a) sometimes the Sages will be informed that one particular subject is to be compared to another, but the two similar words which actually comprise the *gezeirah shavah* are left to them to identify; (b) sometimes the Sages will be aware of the two similar words to be used for the *gezeirah shavah,* but must locate the appropriate contexts in the Torah *(Halichos Olam).*

An example of an instance in which the Sages received only the subject-contexts: It is stated in the case of a *na'arah* (generally, a girl between the ages of twelve and twelve-and-a-half) who is raped: אֲשֶׁר לֹא אֹרָשָׂה, *who is not betrothed* [i.e., has not had *erusin*] *(Deut.* 22:28). The same words are found also in the case of a betrothed *na'arah* who is seduced *(Ex.* 22:15). Just as in the case of rape the fine is fifty silver coins, so, too, in the case of seduction; and just as in the case of seduction the coins must be *shekels,* likewise in the case of rape they must be *shekels* (*Kesubos* 38a). The *Gemara* then proceeds to debate whether the aforementioned *gezeirah shavah* should be based on another word — בְּתוּלָה, *virgin* — found in both verses, or on *who is not betrothed,* as stated. From this debate it is clear that the Sages of the Talmud had received a tradition from their teachers that the subjects of rape and seduction should be compared to each other by way of a *gezeirah shavah,* but that they were never told which two words actually comprised the *gezeirah shavah.* Thus, the Talmudic dialectic seeks to discover the proper similar words *(Halichos Olam).*

An example of when the Sages received only the similar words: It is written regarding a master's obligation to give presents to his Jewish bondman upon completion of the latter's service: תִּתֵּן לוֹ, *You shall give him* ... *(Deut.* 15:14). Of one whose ox has gored a gentile slave, the Torah says: ... יִתֵּן לַאדֹנָיו, *he shall give to the master* ... *(Ex.* 21:32). By way of *gezeirah shavah* from the similar words *give,* the *Gemara* essays to ascribe a value of thirty shekels to the Jewish bondman's present, similar to the amount of damages paid to the master of the heathen slave (*Kiddushin* 17a). Then, using the same two similar words, the *Gemara* suggests a *gezeirah shavah,* from another subject-context, (עֲרָכִין, *arachin:* the fixed valuation of an adult man) which would raise the value of the gift to fifty shekels. Thus, we see here that the Sages were aware of the key word — *give* in the case of the manservant — and were charged with finding its counterpart to complete the *gezeirah shavah. Tosafos (Shabbos* 97a, s.v. גזירה) ask why R' Yehudah ben Beseirah, who was not taught a certain *gezeirah shavah* by his teachers, did not nevertheless learn it from his colleagues, and that would also constitute 'receiving it by tradition.' Citing *Rabbeinu Tam,* they answer that the Sages received a tradition regarding the exact number of *gezeirah shavah* interpretations in the Torah, and this one exceeded that amount. Therefore, R' Yehudah did not accept it.

Types of Interpretation

There are three types of *gezeirah shavah* interpretations: (a) *free on both sides* — both of the similar words which comprise the *gezeirah shavah* are superfluous in their respective contexts, for no other interpretation is made from either of them. Thus, both are 'open,' serving no other purpose than to form the *gezeirah shavah;* (b) *free on one side* — either one of the similar words is extra while the other is not; (c) *not free at all* — neither word is superfluous, since both are used for other interpretations.

A *gezeirah shavah* of the first variety, which is free on both sides, is — according to all authorities — an absolute teaching, and even though many distinctions and disparities may be found between the side which teaches and its counterpart, nevertheless, such a *gezeirah shavah* cannot be refuted. Since it is free on both sides, we regard the teaching as one expressly written in the Torah, and for that reason it cannot be challenged.

A *gezeirah shavah* that is free on one side is considered valid only if it cannot be refuted. However, if it can be shown that the side which teaches is either more superior or deficient than the other side, then the *gezeirah shavah* may be rebutted — in much the same manner as a *kal vachomer* is challenged. A second opinion in the *Gemara,* however, maintains that even a *gezeirah shavah* that is free on one side is considered an absolute teaching which cannot be refuted. Thus, according to that opinion, the only practical difference between a *gezeirah shavah* that is free on two sides and one that is free on one side is that when presented with the choice of learning from one or the other, we select the former as the source of the teaching.

A *gezeirah shavah* that is free on neither side is not valid. A second opinion in the *Gemara* disputes this, however, maintaining that such a *gezeirah shavah* is similar to one that is free on one side — that is, it is valid if not successfully challenged. According to this view, the only practical difference between a *gezeirah shavah* that is free on one side and one that is free on neither side is that when presented with the opportunity to learn from one or the other, we select the former as the source of instruction.

To construct a *gezeirah shavah* that is free on both sides, it is unnecessary to have a superfluous word on each side. Even if there are two extra words on one side, each one counting for one of the sides, then this is considered a *gezeirah shavah* that is free on both sides. An example of this would be the *gezeirah shavah* mentioned above, from which we derive that an uncircumcised *Kohen* is prohibited to eat *terumah.* This halachah is based on the phrase תּוֹשָׁב וְשָׂכִיר, *a sojourner and a hired servant,* which appears in connection with both the Pesach sacrifice and the laws of *terumah.* However, these two expressions — *sojourner* and *hired servant* — are extra only in the Pesach context, but in the *terumah* passage they are required for that subject itself *(Yevamos* 70a). In this *gezeirah shavah* the two extra expressions, *sojourner* and *hired servant,* are not identical. However, it is still possible to construct a *gezeirah shavah* for reasons that will be explained in the following paragraph.

Occasionally, a *gezeirah shavah* is formulated even though the extra words are not identical or similar, since they do refer to the same subject matter. In this context the *Gemara (Makkos* 13b, *Menachos* 4a) states: *Returning* and *coming* have the same import. The *Gemara* is referring to the prescribed treatment of a נֶגַע צָרַעַת, *plague of tzaraas* (discoloration; usually, but imprecisely, translated as leprosy), in the walls of a house. Initially, the house is closed up for a week, after which: *And the Kohen shall return on the seventh day and shall see ... (Lev.* 14:39). After another week passes: *And if the affliction returns and breaks out in the house ... Then the Kohen shall come and see ...* (ibid. v. 43). Just as upon his returning (at the conclusion of the first week) the *Kohen* must remove the leprous stones, scrape and replaster, and then close up the house for another week, so, too, upon his *coming* (after the second week) he must remove the stones, scrape and replaster, and wait another week. The *Gemara* asks: What is the *gezeirah shavah?* Here it says *return,* and there it says *come!* Upon which the School of R' Yishmael replied: *Returning* and *coming* have the same import.

Such a *gezeirah shavah,* in which the two extra words are similar only in meaning, is utilized only when there is no alternative *gezeirah shavah* containing two extra, identical words.

'There is no partial *gezeirah shavah.*' This principle is diversely interpreted by the *Rishonim.* Some construe it to mean that every detail of halachah that the side which instructs possesses must be transferred to the other side, and not just the single law being sought. Others understand the rule as requiring each side to transfer its laws to the other, so that the *gezeirah shavah* becomes a bilateral means of instruction *(Yad Malachi).*

After a particular halachah is applied from one subject to another through a *gezeirah shavah,* the question remains as to how the new law is to be treated in a general sense. That is, should this new law be qualified and conditioned by the laws of the subject-context from which it issued, or by the laws of the subject-context to which it is being inferred? The *Tannaim* are, in fact, divided on this issue. Some maintain that since the law was derived from the instructing side, it should be interpreted according to the relevant laws of that subject. Others argue that henceforth the new law should be modified by the relevant laws of the subject-context where it is actually stated.

הֶיקֵּשׁ / Hekesh

Two subjects that are juxtaposed in one Scriptural verse are compared to each other in the manner of a *gezeirah shavah.* This rule of exegesis is termed *hekesh* (analogy). R' Yishmael did not mention it in his list of thirteen rules, since he regarded the *hekesh* as the equivalent of an explicitly written teaching *(Sefer Hakerisus).*

An example of the *hekesh* is found in *Kiddushin* (14b): The *Gemara* states that just as a woman can be acquired for *kiddushin* (the first stage of marriage) with money (ibid. 1:1; see above), she can also be acquired as a bondwoman with money. Through a *hekesh,* we may derive that a Jewish bondman can also be acquired with money. The Torah says: *If your brother shall be sold to you — the Jew or Jewess* ... The Jewish bondman is compared to the Jewish bondwoman. Just as the latter is acquired with money, so, too, is the former.

A *hekesh* cannot be refuted, since it is like an expressly written teaching. In this respect the *hekesh* resembles a *gezeirah shavah* that is free on both sides (see above).

There is no partial *hekesh,* just as there is no partial *gezeirah shavah.*

Whenever one subject can be analogized through a *hekesh* to either of two other subjects, one of which is more lenient and the other more stringent, the *hekesh* is made to the more stringent subject. According to *Rabbeinu Tam,* this rule, when applied to monetary matters, obligates the person in question to pay.

Sometimes, the conjuctive letter (ו), meaning *and,* will connect two adjoining subjects, so that each one can be deduced from the other. This ו' הַמּוֹסִיף *(the* ו *which adds on)* is included in the category of *hekesh (Rashi* to *Zevachim* 48a).

סְמוּכִים / Semuchim

Two consecutive verses may become a source for interpretation. This rule, which resembles the *hekesh,* is supported by the verse *(Psalms* 111:8), *They are* [סְמוּכִים] *steadfast forever, for eternity, accomplished in truth and fairness (Yevamos* 4a; see *Berachos* 10a, *Rashi* ad loc.). This rule is also not included in R' Yishmael's list.

An example of this principle is given in *Yevamos* (loc. cit.): If a *yevamah* falls for *yibum* to a *yavam* who is afflicted with boils, she is not 'muzzled' (i.e., we do not silence her protests against marrying him, and do not force her to do so; rather, we force the *yavam* to allow her to perform *chalitzah* [*Rashi* ad loc.]). This is derived from the juxtaposition of the verses *(Deut.* 25:4*f.): You shall not muzzle the ox when it treads out the grain,* and *When brothers dwell together* ... (the portion regarding *yibum).*

R' Yehudah employs the rule of *semuchim* only when the deduction is obvious because one of the two verses is blatantly out-of-place, or when one of them is superfluous, thereby suggesting a deduction. The statement of the *Gemara (Yevamos* loc. cit.) that R' Yehudah interprets *semuchim* in *Mishneh Torah* (i.e., *Deuteronomy)* does not mean that he refrains from interpreting them elsewhere in the Torah, but that only in *Deuteronomy* were the Sages certain that the verses of all the *semuchim* were either obvious or superfluous *(Tos.* ibid.). However, R' *Betzalel Ranshburg* (ibid.), quoting *Ravan,* maintains that R' Yehudah interpreted *semuchim* only in *Deuteronomy.* This is because the other four books of the Pentateuch were dictated by the Almighty and were not recorded in any particular order, whereas Moses arranged the sections of Deuteronomy in a certain sequence for the purpose of interpreting them.

The *Gemara* (ibid.) gives an example of *semuchim* in which one of the verses is out-of-place and the other is superfluous:

The Torah *(Deut.* 22:11) says: *You shall not wear shatnez* (a mixture of wool and linen). Following that it says: *You shall make twisted cords (tzitzis) for yourself.* Applying the rule of *semuchim,* the Talmud derives that the prohibition of *shatnez* does not apply in the case of the four-cornered garment to which *tzitzis* (fringes) must be attached. This instance of *semuchim* is both *out-of-place* and *superfluous:* It is out-of-place because the verse, *You shall make twisted cords,* should have been included in the passage concerning *tzitzis* (viz., *Num.* 15:37*ff.).* It is superfluous because the Torah already prohibited *shatnez* in the verse, *You shall not drape over yourself a garment of two kinds of material mixed together (Lev.* 19:19).

III

בִּנְיַן אָב / Binyan Av

(General Principle)

When the Torah reveals a law in one passage, that law may be applied to all other cases that logically appear to be similar. This rule of interpretation is called *binyan av* [literally, *the building of the father*], inasmuch as the original source of the law is like an אָב, *father,* and those passages to which the law is applied resemble its offspring *(Halichos Olam).*

The prerequisite for a *binyan av* is that the 'father' and its 'offspring' be similar to one another in at least one aspect of Halachah.

This principle is divided into two categories: (a) A *binyan av* from one verse; (b) a *binyan av* from two verses.

A Binyan Av from One Verse

Some explain a *binyan av* from one verse as a *binyan av* from one source, which the Talmud calls מָה מָצִינוּ, *mah matzinu* (lit., *'what do we find?')* — i.e., just as we find that one particular law possesses aspect A and aspect B, so any other subject which possesses aspect A should also possess aspect B. The Talmud also refers to this method of instruction as חָדָא מֵחָדָא, *one from one.*

Others dispute this definition, arguing that this type of interpretation is not included among R' Yishmael's hermeneutic rules, since such a teaching is as obvious as if it were expressly written in the Torah. Rather, they define *binyan av from one verse* as two subjects from which we can infer a law, because they share a צַד הַשָּׁוֶה, *common feature.*

This works as follows: When it is impossible to compare subject A to subject B with regard to a particular law, because B contains a stringency not found in A and it is conceivable that this stringency is responsible for B's having that particular law, we adduce a second instructive subject C which lacks the stringency of B and yet possesses the particular law with which we are concerned. Thus, C is proof that the stringency in B is not the cause of the particular law in B. Further, should C possess its own stringency which is not found in A, we may adduce proof from B, which also lacks C's stringency, that C's stringency is likewise not responsible for the existence in C of the law we are trying to apply to A. Therefore, we seek an attribute that is common to both B and C, and conclude that this common feature is obviously the cause of the law they both share. If A also possesses this common attribute, then we may successfully apply to it the law found in the other two.

Those who maintain that this is the correct definition of *binyan av* offer proof from the very wording of the term: *binyan* means *a building;* if one places two flat stones on the ground and another on top of them, he has built something that will endure. However, if one places one stone on top of another, what he has built will not endure. [Similarly, a *binyan av* is something derived from two verses, not one.] According to this opinion, it is nevertheless called a *binyan av from one verse* because the two instructive verses are related.

A Binyan Av from Two Verses

According to the first opinion regarding a *binyan av* from one verse, a *binyan av* from two verses is a law derived from two verses and applied to other subjects. According to those who define the *binyan av* from one verse in this manner, a *binyan av* from two verses is a law derived from two totally unrelated verses.

One example of a common-feature interpretation teaches us that whenever the word צַו, *command,* is written in the Torah, the intent is that the commandment should be carried out immediately, i.e., by Moses' generation, but that it is also applicable to all future generations *(Baraisa of R' Yishmael).* This principle is derived as follows:

The Torah *(Lev.* 24:3) describes the commandment to kindle lights in the Temple as חֻקַּת עוֹלָם, *an ordinance forever,* which indicates that the precept is perpetual. It is further written *(Num.* 8:3), *Aaron did so; he lit the lamps ...,* signifying that Aaron discharged this obligation immediately. Regarding the commandment to expel ritually impure persons from the Camp, it says (ibid. 5:4), *The Children of Israel did so; they sent them out* — an immediate fulfillment of the responsibility. To charge future generations with this obligation as well, Scripture (ibid. 19:10) refers to it as *an ordinance forever* (*Ravad,* commentary to *Sifra*).

In connection with both subjects the word צַו, *command,* is written, and thus we infer from them that any other commandment in the Torah which contains this word must also be fulfilled immediately, as well as by posterity. However, it would not be possible to derive this principle solely from the commandment of lighting the Menorah, because it possesses unique stringencies — it is performed regularly and in the inner sanctum of the Temple. Similarly, since the commandment to expel the impure carries the severe penalty of כָּרֵת (spiritual excision, premature death) for its violation, one cannot infer from it to other commandments whose transgressions are not equally punishable. Nevertheless, both do possess the common attribute that the word צו is written in their passages. Hence, any other commandment which shares this attribute will also share their special law — that it must be fulfilled immediately as well as by all future generations.

A common-feature interpretation can be refuted by adducing proof that the two instructive subjects possess another attribute unique to them, so that we cannot infer the law in question to any other subject which lacks this second attribute. However, one cannot challenge a common-feature argument by claiming that the individual stringency of each instructive subject is responsible for the existence of the law, and that since the third subject to which we wish to make an inference possesses neither of these stringencies, this particular law, too, does not apply to it. For if such an argument were valid, it would nullify entirely the common-feature argument, since the very cogency of the argument lies in the fact that each instructive subject has a stringency the other lacks, thereby demonstrating that the law in question is not a result of the stringencies. Even though the *Gemara* does occasionally raise such a refutation, the commentators (to *Kesubos* 32a) have formulated principles to explain these exceptions.

When we wish to refute an inference made from one subject to another through the 'one from one' interpretation (see above), the refutation must be substantial — i.e., that one subject possesses a stringency or leniency not found in the other. However, when the inference is made from two verses through the common feature argument, then even a minimal refutation will suffice. In other words, refuting a 'one from one' argument — be it a *kal vachomer* or a *mah matzinu* (see above) — with the fact that the instructive subject has a certain attribute that the other subject lacks is not a valid refutation if the attribute is insignificant — i.e., neither severe nor lenient in nature. However, when deriving a law from two subjects, any common attribute that the two instructive subjects share — even if it is insignificant — is sufficient to preclude our inferring from them to a third subject which does not possess that attribute *(Halichos Olam).*

This rule is called בִּנְיַן אָב, *binyan av,* (*av* meaning *father*) and not בִּנְיַן אֵם (אֵם meaning *mother*), in contrast to the terms יֵשׁ אֵם לַמִּקְרָא, *the written, unvowelized Scriptural text is primary,* and יֵשׁ אֵם לַמָּסֹרֶת, *the text as traditionally pronounced is primary,*[6] because just as a father interacts with another (the mother) to produce an offspring, so, too, in a common-feature *binyan av* we take a law contained in two subjects and apply it to a third subject. The rules regarding Scriptural texts, on the other hand, reveal a law only in

---

6. [This is a dispute found throughout the Talmud. For example, the Torah (*Lev.* 23:42) states the word בסכת, which is traditionally pronounced בַּסֻּכֹּת, in *sukkos* (booths), but which, unvowelized, reads בַּסֻּכַּת in the singular form. Those who maintain that the written, unvowelized text is primary interpret this as indicating that a *sukkah* need consist only of two complete walls and one partial wall (*Sukkos* 6b).]

the place they are applied and not elsewhere, just as the offspring issues directly from the mother *(Sefer Hakerisus; Halichos Olam).*

שְׁנֵי כְתוּבִים הַבָּאִים כְּאֶחָד
Two Verses Which Mutually Exclude

When the Torah states a law in connection with a subject although it could have been inferred from another one already stated, the intent is to restrict that law to those two situations alone. This is true even if the law could have been deduced only from one of the subjects to the other, but not vice-versa. Accordingly, in order for two subjects to qualify as sources for a common-feature interpretation, it is necessary that the law we wish to apply elsewhere could not have been deduced from one of these subjects to the other *(Halichos Olam).*

There are *Tannaim* who maintain that the fact that a law is superfluously stated in one verse is not sufficient grounds to include it in the category of 'two verses which mutually exclude.' But all agree that if the law is superfluously stated in two verses — i.e., it is mentioned in the Torah three times, two of which are unnecessary — it is included in this category.

Rashi (*Kiddushin* 35a) is of the opinion that this 'two verses ...' rule is not absolutely exclusory; rather, it precludes only the inference to a third subject from the other two through a *binyan av* teaching. Whether or not the third subject will have the law that is possessed by the other two must be independently determined. *Tosafos* (ad loc.), however, maintain that this rule absolutely prevents the third subject from having the law of the other two.

IV-VII
כְּלָלִים וּפְרָטִים
Generalizations and Specifications

(IV) כְּלָל וּפְרָט — *A generalization then a specification:* When a generalization is followed by a specification, the law applies only to the specified case.

For example, the Torah *(Lev.* 1:2) uses the expression מִן הַבְּהֵמָה, *from the beasts,* which is a generalization, since the word בְּהֵמָה refers to wild as well as domesticated animals, and מִן הַבָּקָר וּמִן הַצֹּאן, *from the herd and from the flock,* which is a specification informing us that the Torah designates only domesticated animals *from the herd* (i.e., cows and bulls) and *from the flock* (i.e., sheep and goats) as suitable for offerings; hence, wild animals are excluded by the specification *(Halichos Olam).*

The question then arises: Why did the Torah bother to write the generalization at all, since it teaches us nothing? The answer is that if only the specification were written, it would be subject to the other rules of interpretation, such as the *kal vachomer, binyan av,* or the like. Therefore, it is preceded by a generalization to tell us that the law as stated in the specification is precise and immutable.

Some authorities, however, are of the opinion that the generalization adds a new detail to the law.

(V) פְּרָט וּכְלָל — *A specification then a generalization:* When a specification is followed by a generalization, the intent is that all that is implied in the generalization applies, and there are no exceptions to it.

For example, the Torah (*Ex.* 22:9) use the expressions, חֲמוֹר אוֹ שׁוֹר אוֹ שֶׂה, *a donkey, a bull, or a lamb,* a specification, then וְכָל בְּהֵמָה, *or any animal,* a generalization. The latter adds to the specification, so that every type of animal is included.

Again, the question arises: If the generalization indicates that everything is included, why does the Torah write the specification at all? The answer is that if only the generalization were stated, perhaps some items would be excluded by application of a *kal vachomer, gezeirah shavah* or other rule of interpretation. Since, however, the specification precedes the generalization, the latter is perceived as augmenting the former until everything possible is included in it.

Some authorities, however, maintain that, indeed, the specification comes to diminish the generalization category in one aspect.

(VI) כְּלָל וּפְרָט וּכְלָל — *A generalization then a specification then a generalization:* When a generalization is followed by a specification, which in turn is followed by a generalization, the generalization is qualified — whatever resembles the specification is included, and whatever is dissimilar is excluded. This rule is actually a combination of the two previous rules. In the aspect that whatever resembles the specification is included, it is like a פְּרָט וּכְלָל, and in the aspect that whatever is dissimilar to the specification is excluded, it is like a כְּלָל וּפְרָט (*Halichos Olam*).

An example of a כְּלָל וּפְרָט וּכְלָל is found in *Deuteronomy* 14:26, regarding what items one may buy with the money he used to redeem the second tithe: *You shall give the money for whatever your soul desires,* this is a generalization; *for any of the herd or for any of the flock or for wine,* this is a specification; *or for whatever your soul requests of you,* again, a generalization. Just as the specification particularizes items which reproduce and whose sustenance is drawn from the earth, so, too, any item that reproduces and draws its sustenance from the earth may be purchased with the redemption money in Jerusalem (*Nazir* 35b; *Eruvin* 27b).

Regarding which of the two generalizations in a כְּלָל וּפְרָט וּכְלָל is more important is a topic unto itself, and we shall not pursue it here.

פְּרָט וּכְלָל וּפְרָט — *A specification then a generalization then a specification:* When a specification is followed by a generalization, which in turn is followed by a specification, here, too, the generalization is qualified by what the specification implies. This rule, too, is a combination of the פְּרָט וּכְלָל and the כְּלָל וּפְרָט but is not included in R' Yishmael's Thirteen Rules.

An application of this principle is found in *Numbers* 6:3, regarding a נָזִיר, *Nazirite: He shall abstain from wine and strong drink,* — a specification; *from all that is made of the vine,* — a generalization; *from the kernels even to the husk,* again, a specification. Just as in the specification, the fruit (i.e., the grapes and wine) and the refuse of the fruit (the vinegar) are particularized, so, too, whatever is fruit (e.g., unripe grapes) or refuse of fruit (e.g., wormy grapes) may not be eaten by the Nazirite (*Nazir* 34b). Although this rule appears very similar to the כְּלָל וּפְרָט וּכְלָל, there is one significant difference: The latter principle dictates that every item which bears even one similarity to the specification is included, whereas in the פְּרָט וּכְלָל וּפְרָט the item to be included must resemble the specification in at least two aspects. How significant the resemblance had to be was left for the Sages to determine. Occasionally, they considered several aspects as one.

When two generalizations adjoin one another and are either preceded or followed by a specification, the specification is viewed as being situated between the two generalizations, and the entire construct is considered a כְּלָל וּפְרָט וּכְלָל. This rule, too, is not mentioned in R' Yishmael's list.

An example of such an instance is found in the passage concerning פִּדְיוֹן הַבֵּן, *redemption of the firstborn (Num.* 18:16): *And those who are to be redeemed from a month old,* a generalization; *you shall redeem,* again, a generalization; *according to your valuation, five silver shekels,* a specification. Just as the specification particularizes property that is movable and of intrinsic value, so, too, anything which is movable and of intrinsic value may be used for redeeming the firstborn (*Shevuos* 4b). Although the specification is written after the two generalizations, the Talmud interprets the verse as a כְּלָל וּפְרָט וּכְלָל.

(VII) **כְּלָל הַצָּרִיךְ לִפְרָט, וּפְרָט הַצָּרִיךְ לִכְלָל** — *A generalization which requires a specification, and a specification which requires a generalization.* This rule is to be distinguished from that of a כְּלָל וּפְרָט in which the meaning of both the generalization and the specification is perfectly clear. Thus, in the example cited at the beginning of the chapter the generalization (beasts) is self-explanatory, as is the specification (the herd and the flock), so that there is no need for one to clarify the other. Hence, in the case of כְּלָל וּפְרָט the specification comes not to explain, but to particularize the generalization. However, in the case of כְּלָל הַצָּרִיךְ לִפְרָט, in which the meaning of the generalization is ambiguous, the specification comes only to clarify what was intended by the generalization. The rule is therefore aptly called *a generalization which requires a specification* to explain its meaning.

Regarding the obligation to cover the spilt blood of an animal after slaughtering, the Torah says (*Lev.* 17:13): וְכִסָּהוּ בֶּעָפָר, *he shall cover it with dust.* The *Gemara* (*Chullin* 88b) could have applied the כְּלָל וּפְרָט rule to this verse as follows: *He shall cover it* — a generalization; *with dust* — a specification, and only what is specified applies — that is, only dust may be used to fulfill this duty. However, it rejects this interpretation, since here the specification is necessary to eliminate an ambiguity surrounding the meaning of the generalization, and therefore a כְּלָל וּפְרָט interpretation is precluded. This is because the root of כִּסָּהוּ, *he shall cover it* — כסה (lit., *hide*, see *Gen.* 18:17) — can connote two different means of covering: (a) by placing a vessel over the blood, or (b) by mixing the blood with sand or dust. However, when the Torah writes *with dust* after the generalization, it is explaining that the duty to cover referred to here is accomplished only by mixing the blood with sand or dust.

Conversely, a generalization may be used to clarify the meaning of a specification — the פְּרָט הַצָּרִיךְ לִכְלָל rule.

There are many varying opinions regarding this topic.

רִבּוּי וּמִעוּט / Amplifications and Limitations

There is a second opinion in the Talmud which maintains that the Torah is not interpreted with the generalization-specification methods. Rather, similar interpretations were made in terms of amplification and limitation. Thus, in place of a כְּלָל וּפְרָט they interpret with a רִבּוּי וּמִעוּט, and so forth.

R' Yochanan said: R' Yishmael, who ministered to R' Nechunya ben Hakanah, who expounded the Torah with the principles of generalization and specification, also expounded it with the principles of generalization and specification. R' Akiva, who ministered to Nachum Ish Gam Zu, who expounded the entire Torah on the principles of amplification and limitation, also expounded it on the principles of amplification and limitation (ibid. 26a).

The essential difference between the two methods of interpretation is: In the כְּלָל וּפְרָט the specification is the explanation of the generalization, and therefore only what is specified actually applies. In the רִבּוּי וּמִעוּט, however, the limitation does not define the amplification, as the specification does, but only excludes portions of the whole category. Thus, the amplification suggests every possibility, and the limitation excludes items from that group.

Further, in the פְּרָט וּכְלָל, since the generalization, which comes second, contradicts the specification, every possibility is included. On the other hand, in the מִעוּט וְרִבּוּי, even though the amplification (which follows the limitation) includes everything, the limitation nevertheless excludes at least one possibility, and they do not conflict.

In the כְּלָל וּפְרָט וּכְלָל, the specification defines the first generalization and the law would apply only to the specified use. The second generalization then comes to include any subject which resembles the specification. However, in the רִבּוּי וּמִעוּט וְרִבּוּי the first amplification includes everything, and the limitation excludes any subject not resembling the particularized case. The second amplification then comes to include even those subjects which do not resemble the particularized case. The end result is that the limitation excludes only one case — viz., the most remote one — and the Sages are charged with the responsibility of determining which case that is *(Halichos Olam).*

VIII-XI

דָּבָר שֶׁהָיָה בִּכְלָל

Something That was Included in a Generalization

There are four rules [numbers eight through eleven in R' Yishmael's list of thirteen] of this category:

(VIII) דָּבָר שֶׁהָיָה בִּכְלָל וְיָצָא מִן הַכְּלָל לְלַמֵּד, *something that was included in a generalization, but was then singled out from the generalization in order to teach something.*

(IX) דָּבָר שֶׁהָיָה בִּכְלָל וְיָצָא מִן הַכְּלָל לִטְעוֹן שֶׁהוּא כְעִנְיָנוֹ, *something that was included in a generalization, but was then singled out from the generalization to discuss a provision similar to the general category.*

(X) דָּבָר שֶׁהָיָה בִּכְלָל וְיָצָא מִן הַכְּלָל לִטְעוֹן טֹעַן אַחֵר שֶׁלֹּא כְעִנְיָנוֹ, *something that was included in a generalization, but was then singled out from the generalization to discuss a provision not similar to the general category.*

(XI) דָּבָר שֶׁהָיָה בִּכְלָל וְיָצָא מִן הַכְּלָל לִדּוֹן בַּדָּבָר הֶחָדָשׁ, *something that was included in a generalization, but was then singled out from the generalization to be treated as a new case.*

We will now explain each of these categories:
(VIII) *Something that was included in a generalization, but was then singled out from the generalization in order to teach something, was not singled out to teach only about itself, but to apply its teaching to the entire generalization.*

This means that if the Torah included a certain item in a general statement or category, and that generalization could adequately teach us the pertinent laws regarding a particular item covered by that generalization, and yet the Torah chooses to single out the item and discuss it individually, we must conclude that the particularized detail comes to teach us something new. Sometimes it will teach us about itself as well as the general law, while at other times it will teach only about the general law.

An example of a case which teaches us both about itself and the general law is discussed in *Sanhedrin* 67b:

An אוֹב, *ov*, and a יִדְּעֹנִי, *yidoni*, are included among the sorcerers, regarding whom it says (*Ex.* 22:17): *You shall not allow a sorceress to live.* Nevertheless, they were singled out in the verse (*Lev.* 20:27), *A man or a woman who has a familiar spirit* (ov), *or who is a necromancer* (yidoni), *shall surely be put to death; they shall cast stones at them,* in order to compare other sorcerers to them, and to teach that just as the *ov* and *yidoni* are stoned, so are all other sorcerers stoned. In this example the *ov* and *yidoni,* which are included in the general law of witches, are specifically mentioned in order to establish the penalty of stoning upon them and upon the category as a whole.

An example of a case which teaches us only about the general law is discussed in the *baraisa* of R' Yishmael.

The Torah says (*Lev.* 7:20): *But the soul that eats of the flesh of the sacrifice of* [שְׁלָמִים] *peace-offerings that is for* H*ASHEM* *when his impurity is upon him, that soul shall be cut off.* Now, the peace-offerings are among the holy offerings, for it is written (ibid. v. 37): *This is the law of the elevation-offering, the meal-offering, the sin-offering, the guilt-offering, the inauguration offering, and of the sacrifice of the peace-offering.* Further, the penalty for eating any of the holy offerings in a state of ritual impurity is כָּרֵת, *kares* (excision), as it says (ibid. 22:3): *Any man from any of your seed who approaches the holy offerings, which the Children of Israel sanctify unto* H*ASHEM*, *when his impurity is upon him, that soul* *shall be cut off from before Me.* Nevertheless, the peace-offering was singled out — not to teach something about itself — but to teach about the general category of holy offerings: just as the peace-offering is in the class of offerings that are invested with the holiness of the Altar — i.e., an offering that has been dedicated as a sacrifice — so, too, the only offerings, whose consumption while in a state of impurity is punished by *kares,* are those which are invested with the holiness of the Altar — thereby excluding those offerings which are consecrated only for the בֶּדֶק הַבַּיִת, *Temple* maintenance. In this illustration, the specification does not teach something about itself, since as a member of the general category of holy offerings it carries the penalty of *kares* regardless; rather, its sole purpose is to teach us about the general category — that offerings of lesser holiness are not included therein.

The question arises why we do not apply the כְּלָל וּפְרָט rule to our example, thereby attaining a markedly different result — that only for eating the peace-offering sacrifice while impure does one receive the *kares* penalty, but not in the case of any other offering *(Halichos Olam). Rashi* (*Shevuos* 7a) answers that the כְּלָל וּפְרָט rule is only applied when the generalization and the specification are juxtaposed but not when they appear in passages far removed from one another in the Torah. *Middos Aharon* writes that when the particular law is never actually mentioned with regard to the specification, but only in connection with the generalization, then we adopt the כְּלָל וּפְרָט rule, whereby the entire general category is reduced to the particularized case. However, when the law is mentioned in connection with both the generalization and the specification, the particularized case is not seen as reducing the general category, for if so the Torah would not have bothered to repeat the halachah in the specific case, after it is already stated in the generalization. Therefore, we must conclude that the specification comes to teach us a fact about the general category.

(IX) *Something that was included in a generalization, but was then singled out from the generalization to discuss a provision similar to the general category, has been singled out to be more lenient rather than more severe.*

This rule stipulates that if a certain item was included in a general category, and then was again mentioned with regard to one of the legal provisions of the general law, or if the new provision bespeaks a leniency for the specified detail, then this item is specified for purposes of leniency, and is not given the stringencies of the general law.

[Although the formulation of this rule states 'to be more lenient rather than more severe,' the converse also holds true.] If the item is specified for purposes of stringency, it is not given the leniencies of the general law.

This rule differs from the former one in that in the previous rule the particularized detail coincides in all its legal aspects with the general law; thus, we conclude that it teaches us something about the general law, providing details not found in the general law. In this rule, however, the specified item varies from the general law, either because only some of the laws of the general law were said regarding it, or because it was specifically singled out as being more lenient or stringent than the general law *(Sefer Hakerisus).*

An example of this category is found in the *Baraisa of R' Yishmael:*

The Torah writes (*Lev.* 13:18): *The flesh, which in the skin thereof was an inflammation, and is healed.* This verse introduces the passage dealing with the affliction termed שְׁחִין, *shechin,* which appears on the flesh after the inflammation caused by a blow heals. Further (v. 24), it is stated: *Or if there is any flesh in the skin where there is a part burnt by fire.* [Here the Torah discusses the affliction called מִכְוַת אֵשׁ, *michvas eish,* which can develop on the skin where burnt flesh has healed.] Scripture thus specifies two types of צָרַעַת, *tzaraas* (loosely, *leprous afflictions*) — *shechin* and *michvas eish* — and was not content merely to include them in the general law of *tzaraas* (ibid., v. 2): *When a man shall have in the skin of his flesh a rising, a scab, or a bright spot, and it is in the skin of his flesh as an affliction of tzaraas.* Had the Torah included them in this verse, these two types of *tzaraas* would have had all the stringencies and leniencies of the general law. However, now that they are individually treated in separate passages, and, furthermore, are expressly exempted from two legal stringencies found in the general law,[7] they are regarded as being specified for purposes of leniency

7. The two exemptions are: (a) Although in the other afflictions raw flesh is considered a sign of impurity, in *shechin* and *michvas eish* it is not. (b) Regarding

and therefore have all the lenient laws which belong to the other types of *tzaraas* in the general category, even though these leniencies were not specified in the separate passages of *shechin* and *michvas eish (Yavin Shemuah).*

(X) *Something that was included in a generalization, but was then singled out from the generalization to discuss a provision not similar to the general category, has been singled out to be both more lenient and more severe.*

This rule states that if a certain item was included in a general category, and was then specifically mentioned with a completely different set of laws than that exhibited by the other items in the general category, then this particularized item receives neither the stringencies nor the leniencies of the general law, but only the laws delineated in its own passage in the Torah.

Example: The Torah states (*Lev.* 13:29): *If a man or a woman has an affliction on the head or the beard* ... Even though these two afflictions of the skin are implied in the general law of *tzaraas,* the Torah nevertheless singles them out to tell us that they have neither the stringency of the general category, regarding which white hair in the affected area is a symptom of impurity, and here it is not, nor the leniency of the general category — that is, *tzaraas* of the head and beard is indicated by the appearance of yellow-colored hair, while in the other forms of *tzaraas* it is not *(Baraisa of R' Yishmael).*

In sum, the essential difference between this rule and the previous one (IX) is as follows: When what is written about the specified item is partially similar to the general law, then the item remains in the general category and has its leniencies [or its stringencies]. This is the previous rule. But when what is written about the specified item is at variance with the general law, then the item is, in effect, excluded from the general category, having neither its stringencies nor leniencies. This is the rule discussed here (X).

---

the other afflictions, if — upon the initial examination by the *Kohen* — no sign of ritual impurity was ascertained, the person was secluded for one week and then reexamined. If the affected area of skin had not spread, he was secluded for another week. Upon a third examination, if the affliction continued to remain in place, the man was declared ritually clean *(tahor).* However, in the cases of *shechin* and *michvas eish* a second confinement was not required; if at the end of the first week the affliction had not spread, the man was immediately declared ritually clean.

(XI) *Something that was included in a generalization, but was then singled out from the generalization to be treated as a new case, cannot be returned to its generalization unless Scripture returns it explicitly to its generalization.*

This rule states that if a certain item was included in a general category, and was then specifically mentioned in connection with a new law that contradicts the general law, then the terms of the general law can no longer apply to the item unless the Torah expressly declares that they do. However, if the purpose of specifying the item is only to invest it with a law not otherwise found in the general law, the item is not considered a new case, since it does not actually contradict the general law *(Halichos Olam).*

An example of this is discussed in the *Baraisa of R' Yishmael* and in *Yevamos* (7a): *And he shall slaughter the he-lamb in the place where they slaughter the sin-offering and the burnt-offering, in the place of the Sanctuary; for as the sin-offering ... so is the guilt-offering* (*Lev.* 14:13). The male lamb referred to here is the guilt-offering of the *metzora* (one afflicted with *tzaraas*). Seemingly there is no need to state, *as the sin-offering ... so is the guilt-offering,* since the place of slaughtering is indicated at the beginning of the verse, while the other regulations concerning this sacrifice are found in the laws of the guilt-offering in *Leviticus* 7; why, then, did the Torah explicitly state: *as the sin-offering ... so is the guilt-offering?* The answer is that since the guilt-offering of the *metzora* was singled out from the general category of guilt-offerings to tell us a new law — that unlike the procedure of other guilt-offerings, here the blood of the sacrifice is applied to the thumb of the *metzora's* right hand and the big toe of his right foot — it might therefore be assumed that this offering requires no placing of the blood and the fat portions of the animal upon the Altar. Therefore, the Torah states explicitly; *as the sin-offering ... so is the guilt-offering,* whereby the specified law is expressly restored to the general law: just as the sin-offering requires placing the blood and fat portions on the Altar, so does the guilt-offering.

It should be noted that the guilt-offering of the *metzora* involves another service not performed with the other guilt-offerings — a wine libation. Yet the *baraisa* we have cited from *Yevamos* does not reckon this detail as a new case, because it is merely an addition to that which is done in connection with the other guilt-offerings.

However, the placing of the blood on the thumb and toe of the *metzora* is considered a new law, since the blood of the other guilt-offerings is entirely poured out on the Altar. Since this requirement contradicts the general law, it is adjudged a new case (see *Tosafos* to *Yevamos* 7a, s.v. לפי).

The question now arises; What is actually the difference between this rule and the previous one (X)? In both, the specified case is legally defined only by the content of its individual passage in the Torah.

To be sure, rules X and XI reach the identical conclusion; however, they essentially involve two strikingly different situations. In the example given in the previous rule (X), an affliction on the head or beard might conceivably be seen as a type of impurity fundamentally distinct from those subsumed under the general law; therefore, we say that it is removed from the general category completely. However, the rule in this section teaches that even though the specified case (in our example, the *metzora's* guilt-offering) is essentially compatible with the other cases (the other guilt-offerings), nevertheless, since a new law is stated regarding it in a separate passage in the Torah, its entire legal content is restricted to what is written in that passage alone — until Scripture expressly returns the specified case to the general category. Even though it would have been possible to deduce rule X from rule XI, nevertheless, since there exists a characteristic distinction between the two situations, R' Yishmael enumerated them separately (*Ravad; Halichos Olam*).

XII

דָּבָר הַלָּמֵד מֵעִנְיָנוֹ וְדָבָר הַלָּמֵד מִסּוֹפוֹ

Elucidation of a Matter from its Context or from a Subsequent Statement

An ambiguous word or passage in the Torah may be explained in one of two ways: (a) from the general context in which it appears (i.e., from the nature of the adjoining subject); or (b) from a subsequent statement in that very passage. The authorities are divided as to whether these two methods should be regarded as separate rules of interpretation or only as one.

(a) The rule of *elucidation by context* is explained in *Sanhedrin* (86a):

The Torah states (*Ex.* 20:15): לֹא תִגְנֹב, *You shall not steal.* The Sages derive from the context that the theft in question must be a capital offense, since the injunction against stealing is preceded by the commandments not to kill and not to commit adultery, which are both capital offenses (*Rashi* ad loc.). The only theft for which someone can receive the death penalty is kidnaping a fellow Jew and treating him like a slave.

In like fashion, the rule of interpretation by context may be employed to resolve an apparent contradiction between a רִבּוּי, *amplification*, and a מִעוּט, *limitation*, that appear in the same verse.

An example of this is discussed in *Kiddushin* 37a (see *Rashi* ad loc.):

These are the statutes and the judgments which you shall observe to do in the land ... (*Deut.* 12:1). One might have thought that the commandments are binding only in the land; the verse therefore continues (ibid.): *all the days that you live upon the earth.* One might have thought that all commandments must be performed both within and without the land; therefore, Scripture specifies: *in the land.* Since the Torah both extends and limits the scope of the commandments, we must look at what is stated further in that passage (v. 2): *You shall utterly destroy all the places where the nations worshiped.* Just as the destruction of idolatry is singled out as a personal duty and is obligatory both within and outside the land, so every personal duty is incumbent both within and outside the land.

Even R' Yehudah, who does not base interpretations upon the juxtaposition of subjects except when one is superfluous or out-of-place (see p. 135), utilizes the rule of interpretation by context. This is because the rule of adjoining subjects yields an entirely new law, whereas interpretation by context merely explains an ambiguity in the text, and even R' Yehudah concedes that for this purpose it is unnecessary for the subject to be superfluous or out-of-place, since the two rules function altogether differently *(Yavin Shemuah).*

(b) The rule of elucidation by subsequent statement works as follows:

And I put the affliction of tzaraas in a house of the land of your possession (*Lev.* 14:34). The verse implies that a house made of stone, wood, and mortar can become ritually impure *(tamei)*. One might think that even a house not made of these materials can become *tamei* — therefore it is later stated (v. 45): *And he shall pull down the house — its stones, its wood, and all the mortar of the house.* Thus, we learn from the conclusion of the passage that only a house constructed with these materials may become *tamei.*

Ravad poses the question that this rule is the same as the כְּלָל וּפְרָט (above #IV) in which case a subsequent specification qualifies the earlier generalization. He answers that in the case of כְּלָל וּפְרָט, the specification comes only to teach something about the generalization. However, in the case of subsequent expression the specification comes primarily to introduce another law. In our example the later verse tells us that the wood and the mortar themselves become *tamei* by the *tzaraas* of the stones. Only incidentally does the verse clarify the ambiguity at the beginning of the passage.

Although this rule is termed *elucidation by a subsequent statement,* it also encompasses an explanatory expression at the *beginning* of a passage. However, in such a case there is no ambiguity, since the explanation of what is to follow is already revealed. Therefore, R' Yishmael, when formulating this rule, chose the example of an ambiguity followed by its explanation. Nevertheless, it goes without saying that if the clarification appears initially, it may certainly be used to explain a subsequent statement *(Middos Aharon).*

XIII

שְׁנֵי כְתוּבִים הַמַּכְחִישִׁים זֶה אֶת זֶה

Reconciling Two Contradictory Verses

The final rule of exegesis in the *Baraisa of Rabbi Yishmael* begins as follows: ... וְכֵן שְׁנֵי כְתוּבִים הַמַּכְחִישִׁים זֶה אֶת זֶה, *Similarly, if two verses contradict one another* ... The term, *similarly,* suggests a connection with the previous rule — i.e., 'a matter elucidated from its context, or from the following text; and similarly, a matter derived from two contradictory verses.' In this case the Sages were empowered to decide between the verses and the Torah requires us to follow their determinations[8]. However, use of a third verse to reconcile two other conflicting verses is not reckoned as one of the rules of exegesis, since the explanation is expressly provided by the third verse *(Tosefos Haazarah).*

An example of a reconciliation made by the Sages is found in *Berachos* (25a):

R' Yonasan contrasted two verses: It is written (*Deut.* 23:13), *And you shall have a place outside of the camp, where you shall go out;* here the Torah did not require that their waste be covered. However, the next verse states: *And you shall have a wedge on your weapon ... and you shall dig with it ... and you shall cover that which comes from you.* How are these two statements reconciled? One speaks of feces, the other of urine.

An example of a *reconciliation by a third verse* is found in the *Baraisa of R' Yishmael:*

One verse states (*Num.* 7:89): *And when Moses had come into the Tent of Meeting to speak with Him,* and another verse states (*Ex.* 40:35): *And Moses was not able to come into the Tent of Meeting.* The third verse (actually the continuation of the second verse) comes to resolve the conflict: *because the cloud dwelled thereon.* From here you can deduce that whenever the cloud was there, Moses did not enter the Tent, but when the cloud departed he entered and spoke with God.

---

8. *R' Shimshon ben R' Zadok,* a student of *Maharam of Rothenburg,* in his *Tashbatz* (§214) offers another explanation of the word וְכֵן. He quotes his teacher: If R' Yishmael wanted to use the word וְכֵן, *similarly,* he would have prefaced each rule after the first with that word. Rather, the meaning of the word here is וְכָאן, *and here,* referring to *Leviticus,* since the Sifra — which begins with R' Yishmael's rules — is written on *Leviticus.* R' Yishmael means to say וְכָאן, *and here* — i.e., at the beginning of *Leviticus* — we find the rule regarding two contradictory verses, for here it is written (1:1): *And HASHEM spoke to him from the Tent of Meeting,* while in another place (*Ex.* 25:22) it says: *And I spoke with you from above the Ark-cover.* A third verse (*Num.* 7:8a) subsequently comes and reconciles the others: Actually, the voice issued from between the two Cherubs on the Ark-cover, but Moses heard the voice only from the Tent of Meeting.

Although the word וְכָאן is written here without an *alef,* it is spelled that way in many other places as well. (We also find it spelled thus in the Mishnah: *Kelayim* 3:2 and *Kinnim* 2:5.)

Addenda

The Number of Rules

We have numbered the rules above in accordance with the phrase 'Through thirteen rules is the Torah elucidated' which opens the *Baraisa* of *R' Yishmael.* Nevertheless, a cursory count will reveal that sixteen are listed. The numbering follows *Raavad* who explains that any two rules which function in a similar manner are regarded as one. Thus, a *binyan av* from one verse and a *binyan av* from two verses are considered one rule. *A generalization which requires a specification,* and *a specification which requires a generalization* are one rule. *Interpretation by context* and *interpretation by subsequent expression* are likewise regarded as one rule. Some have written that rules VIII through XI should actually be regarded as one rule, since each one involves an item which was first included in a general category and was then singled out. This comprehensive rule would consist of four aspects, each with its own set of regulations, but would still be considered one rule *(Tosefos Haazarah).*

Hillel's Rules

The *Baraisa of R' Yishmael* tells us: Hillel the Elder expounded seven rules of interpretation before the elders of Beseira: (1) *kal vachomer,* (2) *gezeirah shavah,* (3) *binyan av* (according to *Raavad's* version), (4) two contradictory verses, (5) generalization and specification (6) *mah matzinu,* a similarity found in another place, and (7) interpretation by context.

Hillel certainly did not intend to dispute the teaching of R' Yishmael, who listed thirteen rules. Some explain that when he expounded before the elders of Beseira, he required only these seven rules, and therefore explained them. Others comment that Hillel chose to condense the thirteen rules of R' Yishmael into these seven.

R' Eliezer Son of R' Yose of Gallilee's Rules

It was taught in a *baraisa* (cited in *Maharzu's* introduction to *Midrash Rabbah*): Wherever you find the words of R' Eliezer [some read: R' Elazar] the son of R' Yose of Galilee, in any topic of *Aggadah* (the homiletical portion of the Talmud), make your ear like a hopper, because it says: *So that you incline your ear toward wisdom.* R' Eliezer, the son of R' Yose of Galilee, says: The Torah is interpreted with thirty-two rules.

In his list of thirty-two rules, R' Eliezer enumerates six which appear in R' Yishmael's *baraisa.* They are: *kal vachomer, gezeirah shavah, binyan av, generalization and specification, something that was in a generalization and was then singled out,* and *two contradictory verses.* Why R' Yishmael did not reckon all the rules in R' Eliezer's list is discussed by the early authorities. They write that since some of R' Eliezer's rules achieve what amounts to explicit Scriptural teachings, R' Yishmael did not include them, since he was interested only in principles of hermeneutical interpretation. Still other rules in R' Eliezer's list pertain to the exposition of Aggadic material, and R' Yishmael was primarily concerned with interpreting texts of a legal nature. Suffice it to say that this complex topic requires a good deal more discussion and clarification.

Likewise, let us point out another relevant principle: In the laws of *Kodashim* (dealing with offerings) a legal conclusion derived by one of the rules of exegesis cannot form the basis for another interpretation. Regarding this, however, several distinctions may be made, and they are explained in Tractate *Zevachim* (50b).

This volume is part of
THE ARTSCROLL SERIES®
an ongoing project of
translations, commentaries and expositions
on Scripture, Mishnah, liturgy,
the classic Rabbinic Writings and thought.

For a brochure of current publications
visit your local Hebrew bookseller
or contact the publisher:
Mesorah Publications, Ltd.
1969 Coney Island Avenue
Brooklyn, New York 11223
(718) 339-1700